The Political Philosophy of St. Robert Bellarmine

An Examination of Saint Cardinal Bellarmine's
Defense of Popular Government
and the Influence of His Political Theory
upon the Declaration of Independence

By Rev. Fr. John Clement Rager, S.T.D.

The Political Philosophy of (then) Blessed (now Saint) Robert Bellarmine by Father John C. Rager, was first published in 1926.

This authoritative 1995 edition has been newly typeset in a modern, compact font and contains the entire text of the 146 page original, complete and unabridged.

ISBN 1-888516-00-3

Published by the Apostolate of Our Lady of Siluva
P.O. Box 4787, Spokane, WA 99202-0787

For information on discounts for quantity purchases of wholesale copies of this book, write to the address above.

NIHIL OBSTAT.
Indianapolis, May 15, 1926
JOSEPH HAMILL, PhD. *Censor Deputatus*

IMPRIMATUR
Indianapolis, May 15, 1926.
†JOSEPH CHARTRAND, *Episcopus Indianapolitanus*

Author's Dedication
As a token of reverence, loyalty and gratitude, this book is dedicated to: THE RIGHT REVEREND JOSEPH CHARTRAND, D.D. Bishop of Indianapolis by the author, John Clement Rager.

PREFACE

If modern civilization is, as historians and others so frequently assert, the fruit of a series of revolutions, then the greater part of the civilized world is still in the throes of one of these, namely, the Social Revolution. For most nations that can lay claim to progress, democracy, in some form, seems to be the goal of all political activity.

The rapid changes in the institutional life of all nations and peoples during the last century have demanded a radical adjustment in their governmental methods and technique, and a thorough sifting of the principles on which states may be established with some hope of promoting the peace and prosperity of their citizens. Successful experiments in popular control of government have strengthened the natural instinct of men towards democratic institutions.

Political democracy seems to hold out most promise for the successful life of society in the future, and, hence, it is of more than passing importance to trace to their source the principles on which democracy has won its way to the confidence of the peoples of the present. We are not here engaged in an analysis of political theory or political philosophy in general, but we may be permitted to remark that a valid criterion of the value of any theory of the state or politics may be found in the wider philosophy of which it is an integrant unit. On few subjects of interest to the historian or the political philosopher is there more uncertainty or confusion than on that of the sources of modern democracy.

Among the many views which have been expressed on the subject none is more ludicrous or so far from the truth as that which would assert that the idea of democracy is entirely a product of modern times. Sectarian polemics and doctrinaire theory, usually at war with existing institutions, are not slow to claim credit for what they are equally eager to change or to destroy.

The modern world neither discovered nor invented Democracy, and the fact is that, if democracy is to retain possession of the progress it has already made, it needs to be on its guard against the enemies which have been raised up by the perversion of what is best in popular control of government as witnessed by certain recent developments in political thought.

The truth is that democracy had its exponents and defenders in the earliest Christian age, in the Middle Ages, and long before the sixteenth century. The truth is that royal autocracy and not democracy was, in general, the political theory of the religious dissenters from the ancient Church in that century. The truth is that at the very time when these innovators are alleged to have emancipated the world, they really enslaved it to absolute and unlimited royal power.

The truth is that the ancient Church, which is often depicted as retarding modern enlightenment, liberty, and democracy, was the very agency which produced the great protagonists of democracy in the period of its greatest danger and saved out of the democracy of the Middle Ages what might be termed the seed thought for the resowing and growth of democratic principles and practice among the nations of modern times.

One of the most prominent defenders of democracy in the late sixteenth and early seventeenth centuries was the illustrious Jesuit Cardinal, the now Blessed Robert Bellarmine. The beatification of Cardinal Bellarmine May 13th, 1923, has brought into well deserved prominence a saint and a scholar whose voluminous writings may stand beside those of St. Thomas Aquinas, and are well worth the closest study. While Cardinal Bellarmine is extensively quoted by political as well as by ecclesiastical writers, we are not aware of any extensive exposition of his political doctrine.

The study of the political tenets of so saintly and learned a man appealed to the author as both interesting and practical. Cardinal Bellarmine's political philosophy is interesting as a simple and clear, logical and reasonable exposition of that type of government which men like to call popular and democratic.

If for no other reason, it is enlightening as original evidence that the sources of world democracy are to be found, not in the political doctrine of the Reformation, but in the writings of Catholic thinkers like Bellarmine. His philosophy is practical for the guidance it affords every man who is entrusted with the welfare and direction of men. It is admirable for its well-balanced theory, for its avoidance of all extremes, for its firmness of principle, for the prudence of action constantly commended and for its justice to all men, ruler and ruled.

Encouraged by those who had read the first draft of this treatise, that a fuller exposition of the political doctrine of this saintly priest of three hundred years ago might be of interest and value to the more serious reader of today, the author has consented to bring his labors to the light of print. He lays no claim to originality in this work. He has merely made a thorough search of all the writings of Cardinal Bellarmine and brought under their respective heads, his various political utterances in their political and historical settings.

The author hereby acknowledges an inestimable debt of gratitude to the Theological Faculty of the Catholic University, especially to the Very Reverend Doctor Patrick J. Healy for his whole-hearted encouragement, direction, and friendship. To his beloved Bishop, The Right Reverend Joseph Chartrand, D.D., of the Diocese of Indianapolis, who graciously allowed time and opportunity to pursue this course of study at the Catholic University of America, and who has ever been a source of spiritual and intellectual inspiration, the author hereby dedicates this work, in sincere appreciation and gratitude.

TABLE OF CONTENTS

INTRODUCTION

"In a commonwealth all men are born naturally free; consequently, the people themselves, immediately and directly, hold the political power so long as they have not transferred this power to some king or ruler."[1] "This tenet," wrote Robert Filmer, private theologian for James I of England, "was first hatched in the schools and hath been fostered by all succeeding papists."[2]

"The most sacred order of kings is of Divine Right." This was the declaration of the *Constitutions and Canons of the Church of England.*

The two preceding declarations contain the pith and marrow of the two outstanding political theories that contended for supremacy in the late sixteenth and early seventeenth centuries. The first was the pronouncement of Cardinal Bellarmine and the traditional view of the Mediaeval Church. The second was the new theory of the "Divine Right of Kings," the accepted political doctrine of the Church of England and of the majority of Protestant religious leaders of the sixteenth century.

The causes which brought to issue such acute opposition of political theory at the close of the Middle Ages were principally three: first, the political power and influence which accumulated in the Papacy throughout the Middle Ages; second, the gradual yielding of feudalism to nationalism, especially from the thirteenth to the seventeenth century; third, the politico-religious upheaval of the sixteenth century.

PAPAL POWER

The first contributing cause must be traced to the very dawn of the Middle Ages, to the conversion of Constantine and to the subsequent long struggle regarding the relations of Church and State. It is the story of the rise, growth, influence and decline of the temporal power of the Popes.

As the prestige and sway of "Old Rome" yielded to the ascending domination of the "New Rome" on the Bosporus, another power, that of the Papacy, came into prominence upon the banks of the Tiber. In Mediaeval tradition the "Donation of Constantine" was alleged at least to have granted to Pope Sylvester, Bishop of Rome, the kingly dignity and crown, imperial robes, temporal sovereignty over Rome and the provinces, towns and castles of all Italy. After the breakdown of the Western Roman Empire, the Church is conceded to have been the only power remaining that could stay the destruction of the invading hordes.

By constant effort to Christianize, civilize, and educate, she conquered the conquerors. The intervention of a Leo the Great, Gregory the Great, Gregory II, Zacharias, or Stephen is well known. The Emperor in the East apparently

---

[1] Cardinal Bellarmine: "In terrena Republica nascuntur omnes homines naturaliter liberi ac proinde potestatem politicam immediate ipse populus habet, donec eam in regem aliquem non transtulerit." *De Clericis*, Ch. VII.

[2] *Patriarcha*, Ch. I.

unconcerned as to the fate of the West and his Exarchate of Ravenna being weak, the Popes began to be looked upon as the natural rulers and defenders of Italy. In 756 Pepin, on petition of Pope Stephen, repelled the Lombards and made the Pope an independent and direct temporal sovereign. On this point Carlyle remarks, "Any one who studies the papal correspondence and the "Liber Pontificalis" in the eighth century will, we think, feel that the leadership of the Roman *Respublica* in the West was forced upon them rather than deliberately sought."[3]

Papal power was effectively increased when on Christmas day of the year 800, the great and powerful Frankish king, Charlemagne, at the head of a solidly Catholic people, aligned himself with the Father of Christendom, Leo III, to reestablish the ancient glory of the Roman Empire and to realize the Mediaeval ideal of a universal and united Christian state of Europe. Not by conquest, but by proclamation of the Pope did Charlemagne receive his title, "Great and Pacific Emperor of the Romans."

Universal empire of unity, peace, and strength had been the ideal of ages past. It was attempted by Alexander the Great, who endeavored to weld the East and the West. It was very nearly realized in the ancient Roman Empire under the masterful statesmanship of Julius Caesar and Augustus. It again came to the fore as the Christian ideal of mediaeval political aspiration in the alliance of Charlemagne and Leo. The Pope and Canon Law governed in the one field; the Emperor and Feudal Law, in the other.

In this universal Christian empire it was not deemed necessary for political unity to annihilate the various small nations and to destroy their individuality; rather were their rights, freedom, and independence to be placed under the protectorate of the Mediaeval Roman Emperor. Spiritually, there never was any question of the idealism and necessity of Christian unity. The idea of combining the civil and ecclesiastical in a world-wide commonwealth did not, by any means, imply that the civil and the ecclesiastical were regarded, even theoretically, as identical. On the contrary the nature and scope of each was carefully defined. Invasion of the spiritual field by the secular arm was opposed as vigorously as the assumption of civil authority by ecclesiastics.

Because, however, no hard and fast line can be drawn between the civil and the religious, and because, in fact, the two spheres so often touch or even overlap, effective cooperation, mutual support, and close association were looked on as the ideal relationship. The primary principle of effective cooperation was that each power is supreme in its own sphere. The ecclesiastic owed allegiance to the king in secular matters, the king owed allegiance to the Church in spiritual matters. In a direct comparison, the dignity of the priesthood was considered the greater, for it was by the priest that the king was consecrated.

Seven centuries later, divine right theorists would endeavor to invert this

---

[3] *History of Mediaeval Political Theory,* Vol. I, p. 289.

order.[4] For seven centuries, until 1530, the Pope, by mutual agreement, crowned the Emperor with a ceremony that inspired reverence and obedience to civil authority. The Emperor in his coronation oath promised to protect and defend the rights and possessions of the Church; he pledged himself to govern according to the laws of justice respecting the rights, dignities, and properties of every subject of the state.

For abuse of this trust, it was admitted that the Pope should have power and right to censure and correct, in extreme cases, even to declare an autocratic king or emperor deposed. In mediaeval thought the priest was responsible to see that the secular ruler did his duty.

As spiritual head in this Christian state and as supreme arbiter over the consciences of men, the Pope was often called upon to administer justice in temporal matters. The Roman Curia served as the highest court of appeals. The papacy came to be recognized as a kind of international, interstatal tribunal, where differences between ruler and ruler or between ruler and subject might be adjusted. The papal power in Europe reached its zenith in the reigns of Gregory the Great (1073-1085), Innocent III (1198-1216), and Boniface VIII (1294-1303). After Boniface it commenced to decline. The circumstances of this diminution of papal influence made possible the great upheaval in the sixteenth century.

While particular instances of absolutism on the part of individual Pontiffs may be recorded, Lecky states that this power, exercised by the Popes in the Middle Ages, was "on the whole favorable to liberty."[5]

This freely recognized power and supreme position of the Pope proved to be a great check upon autocratic rulers. According to traditional mediaeval political theory, too, the ruler held his authority by the consent of the people, and the people found the strongest protector of their rights in the Popes. The more remote beginnings of the theory of the Divine Right of Kings can be traced to conflict, not between Church and State, as Figgis remarks,[6] but between the officials of Church and State, between the *"sacerdotium"* and the "regnum." Civil law and Canon law harmonized well enough.

The Pope claimed his power by direct grant of Christ to St. Peter. The king then found it necessary to frame a counter theory which derived his power as immediately and directly from God. The theory, later known in history as that of the Divine Right of Kings, proclaimed absolute independence of king from Pope and people. It was readily received and fostered by a number of rulers in the sixteenth and seventeenth centuries, which witnessed the great struggle between the theory of Divine Right and Popular Sovereignty.

NATIONALISM AND FEUDALISM

The rise of Nationalism and the corresponding decline of Feudalism, especially from the thirteenth to the seventeenth century, was the second

---

[4] Cf. Carlyle, *History of Mediaeval Political Theories,* Vol. I, pp. 256, 258, 275, 287.

[5] *Rationalism in Europe,* Vol. II, P. 142.

[6] *From Gerson to Grotius,* p. 161.

cause which led up to so pronounced a division of political thought and theory in the sixteenth and seventeenth centuries.

Against the policy of limiting royal power, of expanding popular rights, and of organizing Europe into a universal cosmopolitan Christian empire, there arose a marked tendency among the more powerful rulers to establish national and absolute monarchies. The breakdown of Feudalism aided the movement towards Nationalism. The merchant and craft guilds were disintegrating. The nobles, who had been a great check upon monarchs and an obstacle to national crystallization, were losing their former prestige.

Absolutism seemed to grow more vigorously in the Romance countries where Roman traditions were favorable to monarchy. In France monarchy was slowly forming since the days of Hugh Capet in 987. It took five centuries to unite the petty feudal divisions of France. Ever since the twelfth century, when feudalism was at its zenith, the French lawyers had been striving with united energy to establish a monarchy upon the old foundations of the imperial law of Rome. Nationalism promoted the union of provinces into a single state.

It began in the fourteenth century, by uniting single domains, at times through marriage, and again by conquest. Once united they were passed intact to the eldest son. Since the battle of Crecy, between the French nobles and the English bowmen (in 1346), feudalism began to totter. Monarchy triumphed over feudalism in France under Louis XI (1461-1483), who welded together and rounded out the many French provinces into a national state.

The death of Charles the Bold of Burgandy, in the war with the Swiss, removed the last stronghold of feudal aristocracy. Charles VIII, the son of Louis XI, added Brittany to France, and the king of France was recognized as the "source of law, justice, and order" from Flanders to Spain, from the Rhone to the Ocean. The fourteenth and fifteenth centuries were filled with the tumult of struggle between democracy and chivalry—and monarchy reaped the fruit. Monarchy grew rapidly under Francis I (1515-1547) and culminated in the reign of Louis XIV (1643-1715), who is sometimes quoted as saying, "L'etat c'est moi," "I am the State."

In Spain Ferdinand and Isabella effected a union of Castile and Aragon, Navarre and Granada, and worked towards absolutism by stripping the nobles of their political influences. In 1500 Portugal was an independent national monarchy with its own language. There was no "Cortes" after 1521. In Italy the two Sicilies (i. e. the kingdom of Naples and the island of Sicily) belonged to Spain until 1504 when France obtained rights in Naples, Sicily, and Sardinia. The northern half of Italy was divided into city-states, with Florence a democracy, Milan an aristocracy, Venice an oligarchy, Genoa the possession of France. In the patrimony of St. Peter the Pope was recognized as an Italian prince.

In England we behold the rapid increase of royal power after the War of the Roses, which was destructive to both factions of nobles. The people, tiring of the long drawn out contest and longing for a strong central government to maintain peace, lent their support to the strengthening of monarchy. While the Hundred Years' War (1338-1453) had already drawn distinct national lines between France and England and served to exalt the sense of English nationality and enabled the English king to consolidate his power in the British Isles, the War of the Roses permitted Henry VII in 1485 to emerge from the struggle as King of England and to impose on his country an absolute one-man rule. Royalty gained in power under Henry VIII and Elizabeth until it reached its climax in the accession of James in 1603.

The history of the fifteenth century in Europe concerns itself principally with the process of national coalescence, when smaller states and feudal lordships were grouping themselves into larger nations. At the beginning of the sixteenth century, England, France, Spain, and Portugal were fairly well established monarchies with powerful kings, patriotic peoples, and well developed distinctive languages. Denmark, Norway, and Sweden were kingdoms; Poland, a weak monarchy. In the Holy Roman Empire, we find no such territorial coalition at this time. It consisted of the "Germanies" loosely bound together. Charles V (1521-1553) was too much engaged in extending his territories and in defending them against the Ottomans to find time for thorough internal organization.

The limited mediaeval monarchy was followed immediately not by the modern representative government, but by the absolute monarchy of the sixteenth and seventeenth centuries. Its bearers resented any limitation by pope, council, noble, or popular rights, and became strong protagonists of the Divine Right theory in these centuries. Since then, until the present day, absolute monarchy, while passing away in most instances, has developed an intense spirit of nationalism, which on the one hand has produced much commendable national pride, patriotism, and intensive territorial development; on the other hand, much un-Christian rivalry, national hatred, and the late deplorable World War.

POLITICO-RELIGIOUS REVOLT OF THE SIXTEENTH CENTURY

The third cause which aggravated and accentuated the political differences at this time was the politico-religious revolt against the Papacy in the sixteenth century. While unlimited monarchy was making notable progress for several centuries, one great barrier still obstructed its complete accomplishment. It was the Church of Rome, with her freely recognized traditional right and practice of setting limits to extreme and wanton exercise of political power. The resentment felt by nobles and kings for the restraining power of the Church threw them on the side of Luther when he commenced his campaign of revolt. The active support tendered him by those nobles who were anxious to free themselves from ecclesiastical restrictions Luther reciprocated by "encouraging princely autocracy and by asserting its divine origin and universal competence. Of the princely power then rapidly rising from feudal to sovereign authority he was by temper and circumstance alike an outstanding support."[7] "Rulers," wrote Luther, "are to drive, beat, choke, hang, burn, behead, break upon the wheel, the vulgar

---

[7] *Cambridge Modern History,* Vol. III, p. 739.

masses."[8] "That to the Reformation was in some sort due the prevalence of the notion of the Divine Right of Kings is generally admitted."[9] In supporting this theory the religious dissenters from Rome easily enlisted the favor and protection of a number of temporal rulers of that day.

The political theory underlying the politico-religious revolt in England as effected by Thomas Cromwell under Henry VIII and developed by Burleigh under Elizabeth was Machiavelli's State Utilitarianism by which person, conscience, and goods became subservient to the State and the sovereign. Kings began to declare themselves as equal to the Pope, their sovereignty as of immediate divine right, their kingship as superior and anterior to the priesthood. In accordance with this principle Henry VIII carried the idea of nationalism into the Church; he established a national Church of England and proclaimed himself its spiritual head. Edward VI and Elizabeth issued a Book of Common Prayer. James I forced himself upon the kingdom as its first theologian.

The situation in summary shows that, at the close of the sixteenth century, the power of the Papacy, of the Nobility, and of the People was so weakened that the supporters of royal autocracy, encouraged by the religious defection from Rome, now ventured more boldly to put their theory into practice. Parliaments were dissolved; the tradition of constitutional limitation and representative government was abandoned; the religious and civil rights and liberties of the people were disregarded. The democracy of the Middle Ages was to be relegated to the past. Against this autocracy of kings and abuse of political power, the Catholic Church raised her voice in no uncertain tone and emphatically reasserted both her own religious independence and the rights of the people.

CARDINAL BELLARMINE

The most prominent defender and champion of democracy, of the traditional, popular, and Catholic cause at this time, was the distinguished and learned Jesuit Cardinal, Robert Francis Romulus Bellarmine. Cardinal Bellarmine was unquestionably the most remarkable man of his age. A brief sketch of his life may give a better estimate of the man whose political philosophy will be the subject of our investigation in these pages.

Robert Bellarmine was born October 4th, 1542, in the romantic little town of Montepulciano, which nestles in the Umbrian hills of Italy. Not far from the market place in this quaint mediaeval village stands the Palazzo Tarrugi, which formerly belonged to the family Bellarmine. Here the great Cardinal first saw the light of day and spent his youth. Over the doorway of this Palazzo there is a tablet bearing the following inscription: "In this house was born, October 4th, 1542, the son of the noble Vincenzo of Montepulciano and his wife Cinzia, the sister of Pope Marcellus II, Robert Francis Cardinal Bellarmine; an immortal glory to the Church, to Italy, and to his birthplace; who, by the holiness of his life and the comprehensiveness of his learning,

---

[8] *Sämmtliche Werke* (Erlangen) Vol. XV, p. 276.

[9] Figgis, *Divine Right of Kings*, p. 15.

became the unvanquished champion in the controversies of faith, morals, and Holy Scripture and who, after four hundred years, still engages the admiration of men."

His father was a man of practical Christianity, who, for his active interest in civic affairs, commanded the respect and highest esteem of his townsmen. His mother was a woman of exceptional virtue, charity, prayer, and Christian mortification. Robert was the third son amongst twelve children. Of these, two sons and three daughters dedicated themselves to religion. While practically nothing is known about Bellarmine's brothers and sisters there were few men of his time better known and none more widely honored than this learned Jesuit.

Physically, Robert was not lavishly endowed. He is described by Sir Fynes Moryson in his "Itinerary" thus: "I came into Bellarmine's chamber that I might see this man, so famous for his learning and so great a champion of the Popes; who seemed to me not above forty years old, being leane of body and something low of stature, with a long visage and a little sharpe beard upon the chin, of a browne color, and a countenance not very grave, and for his middle age wanting the authority of grey heires."— "He gently answered, and with gravity, not so much swallowing the praises I gave him, as shewing that my company should be most pleasing to him, commanded his novice that he should presently bring me in, when I should come to visit him."[10]

Despite general ill health, he possessed a very cheerful, vivacious disposition and he exhibited the unusual quality of combining an artistic temperament with a sharp, clear intellect. As a boy he was known for angelic purity, earnestness, and industry. He was beloved by teacher and playmate. At home he would often mount a chair for his pulpit and assume to preach to his brothers and sisters.

At twelve Robert attended lectures in logic. He liked music and poetry and learned to play a number of musical instruments. At the age of fifteen he was chosen to deliver a Latin speech in the public auditorium of his native town. In 1560, September 16th, at the age of eighteen, Robert entered the Jesuit novitiate of Maria della Strada in Rome. At the end of a three years' course, he was designated to defend publicly the whole field of Philosophy for a Master's degree.

According to the practice of the Jesuits, he was now appointed professor at the college of Florence, where he distinguished himself by exceptional teaching ability. In a discourse on the "Praises of Science" in October of 1563, delivered in the presence of the Archbishop of Ragusa, the Bishop of Marsica, and other distinguished churchmen, he excited the profound admiration of all who heard him. A year later he was promoted to Mondovi where throngs of people came to hear him in one of the largest churches of the city.

In the fall of 1567 Bellarmine began his theological studies in Padua, but

---

[10] Rev. Herbert Thurston, S. J., on *Blessed Cardinal Bellarmine*. Catholic Mind, June 22, 1923, reprint from the London "Tablet."

in 1568 the general of the Netherlands Province who was St. Francis Borgia, requested that an able preacher be sent to the university town of Louvain. Bellarmine was furnished a horse and was sent to Milan, from which place he set out for Louvain accompanied by another Jesuit and the English Cardinal Allen.

The University of Louvain numbered no less than three thousand students at this time, and next to that of Paris, was perhaps the most prominent university on the Continent. Here Bellarmine ascended the pulpit of the Church of St. Michael in July, 1569. Speedily his audiences grew into thousands. Learned Protestants from Holland and England journeyed to Louvain and sat at his feet with note book and quill. Many were reconverted to the ancient Church.

These discourses, which were in Latin, were collected and recopied forty years later and reprinted in six editions and several translations. The secret of his success as an orator is described as consisting in the intensity of his zeal, in the conviction of his mind, in the life of his discourse, in the directness of his censures, and in the radiance and light of his countenance.

He possessed a wealth of general information; he had read all the Church Fathers and theologians; and with a thorough knowledge of Church history he combined an exceptional memory for long and difficult quotations. By interweaving interesting incidents, comparisons, examples, dialogues, dramatic repetitions, rhetorical climaxes, he held his audiences spellbound. His proofs were direct, clear, sharp, powerful, convincing. At this time he had not yet received priestly ordination.

In 1570 he was ordained a priest and celebrated his first mass on the Sunday after Easter. During the last six years of his sojourn at Louvain he gave public lectures on the whole Summa of St. Thomas. Seven years Bellarmine spent in Louvain, the field of his first great activity. One hundred and forty years later his memory was held in such veneration that the theological faculty of Louvain petitioned the Pope to beatify this servant of God, "who by his learning and piety worked so ardently for God's Church." In 1713 another petition was sent to Rome stating, "the whole of Belgium preserves with deep gratitude the memory of the Venerable Cardinal Bellarmine and would regard it an honor to see him raised to the rank of sainthood." May 13th, 1923, Cardinal Bellarmine was beatified.

November 26th, 1576, this learned divine ascended the "Chair of Controversy" in Rome, which had recently been founded at the Roman College. He occupied this seat for eleven years. His lectures were received with such acclaim that he was directed by his superior to put them into print. To this he consented very modestly, and in the year 1586, the first volume of his *Controversiae Christianae fidei adversus hujus temporis haereticos* appeared in Ingolstadt. Two years later a second and a third volume appeared; and eight years later, the fourth volume.

The work passed through forty editions. Among his many writings the most notable are these disputations which will ever stand as a witness to his greatness. The renowned church historian, Baronius, wrote, "All the learned awaited ardently and now received and praised most highly these disputations." The work made a profound impression throughout Europe and caused Protestant England and Germany to erect Chairs of learning to refute his arguments.

The renowned Theodore Beza expressed the opinion of those opposed to him: "Hic fiber nos perdidit"—"this book has ruined us." Queen Elizabeth directed that lectures be delivered against him in Cambridge, but instead of refuting Bellarmine these lectures made him more widely known and believed. The professor, Justus Calvin, who studied Bellarmine to refute him, was converted to Catholicism. In 1600 David Paraus, Professor at Heidelberg, opened the College Anti-Bellarminianum to train controversialists to cope with the writings of Bellarmine. Cardinal Dietrickstein of Olmutz exclaimed, "Twenty editions in thirty years; everywhere Bellarmine is read; every word is received and believed as that of an oracle."

The learned Englishman Whitaker (d. 1595) said: "Until now we were ignorant of the true position of the Roman Church. Since Bellarmine has come forward we know exactly what that Church teaches upon every article of faith."[11] Some were unwilling to believe that one man could have been the author of so voluminous and powerful a work. They began to suspect that under the name "Robert Bellarmine" was concealed the whole army of Jesuit theologians. Robert, they said, stood for "robur"—strength; Bellarmine, for "bella"—wars, "arma"—weapons, "minae"—threats.

There were no important Protestant theologians of the seventeenth century who did not attack Bellarmine's writings. A modern critic says of him: "His disputations covered systematically all the prominent issues of the time, theological, ecclesiastical, political, and constituted a formidable arsenal of arguments."[12] Even today Bellarmine's "Controversies" are regarded as the foundation of all modern Apologetics. His work compares well with the Summa of St. Thomas. In a clear, well-defined, and skillful division of his matter, he builds up his arguments step by step with a precision and completeness that leaves little for rebuttal.

This eminent ecclesiastic was entrusted with the highest commissions and most difficult offices in the Church. In October of 1589 he was sent as theological adviser to Cardinal Gaetani in Paris. The chief agent in the revision of the Bible in 1591 was Robert Bellarmine. In 1592 he was made Rector of the Roman College; in 1594, Provincial of the Society of Jesus; and in 1597 Pope Clement VIII called him to Rome and appointed him his private theologian, Examiner of Bishops, and Consultor of the Holy Office. In the Consistory of March 3rd, 1599, Pope Clement VIII declared his intention of raising Bellarmine to the Cardinalate in the following statement: "We have selected him because the Church of God has not his equal in learning." From 1602 to 1605 he labored as Archbishop of Capua.

---

[11]For most of the data on the life of Cardinal Bellarmine, the author is indebted to the splendid work of Emmerich Raitz von Frentz, S. J., *Der ehrwürdige Kardinal Robert Bellarmine, S. J., ein Vorkampfer für Kirche and Papsttum.* Herder & Co., 1921, St. Louis, Mo.

[12]Dunning, *Hist. of Pol. Theories,* p. 128. *From Luther to Montesquieu.*

The next fifteen, the closing years of his life found the Cardinal a staunch defender of every cause in which the interests of religion were at stake. In the Venetian trouble of 1606 he and his friend Cardinal Baronius stood in the forefront of the fray against Friar Paoli Sarpi and a set of theologians called the "Seven Fools of Venice." In the controversy with James I of England over the oath of allegiance, Bellarmaine was again the great protagonist of the persecuted Catholics, and refuted the doctrine of passive obedience. Against the Scotch Jurist, William Barclay, of Angers, France, he defended in 1609 an indirect power of the Pope in temporalities. Against Henry IV, he proclaimed his views on the origin of civil power and denied that this or that particular king ruled by Divine Right.

What was a fixed tradition of the Middle Ages, Cardinal Bellarmine was earnest in his efforts to popularize, namely, the doctrine that power is given by God to the people, and that they in turn commit it to him whom they choose as ruler. For this contention he was proclaimed an anarchist and revolutionist by his opponents. Cardinal Bellarmine well deserves to be hailed the "Patron of True Democracy."[13]

In 1618 he wrote his *De Officio Principis*, which outlined the duties of Christian Princes towards God, the Church, their subjects, and neighboring princes. In this work he displays a thorough knowledge of the habits and dangers at the royal courts of his time.

As the Cardinal approached his eightieth year, Pope Gregory XV released him from all obligations at the Papal Court. In August of 1621 he retired to the quiet of the monastery, where, a few weeks later, on the 17th of September, 1621, he died. The Consistorial Registry contains under the date of September 17th, 1621, the following entry: "Robert Bellarmine, Cardinal priest of Montepulciano and member of the Society of Jesus, passed today at the twelfth hour out of the land of the dead into the realms of the living—an illustrious man, a celebrated theologian, a keen defender of Catholic faith, equally devout, prudent, and generous."

Cardinal Bellarmine had died, but he lives on in the memory of the world, even today, as a defender of truth, as a model of saintliness and, as we shall endeavor to show in this treatise, as the champion and patron of modern democracy.

An estimate of this great Cardinal in summary is the following: As a priest and ecclesiastic, he was lauded by his brother cardinals as the counterpart of a St. Charles Borromeo. As a man of letters and science, there was not his equal among his contemporaries. He occupied with notable success, chairs in Florence, Mondovi, Piedmont, Louvain, and Rome. As an orator he was the marvel of his age, attracting great audiences of both Catholics and Protestants.

As a controversialist, Cardinal Ubaldinus compared him to an Athanasius or an Augustine. By Cardinal Centinus he was referred to as "the pillar of Christain faith" and "the vindicator of Catholic truth." Though unflinching in his arguments, he commanded the respect of his opponents to an unusual degree. In the political life of Europe he was a far-reaching influence and the

---

[13] *Blessed Robert Bellarmine of the Society of Jesus,* Thomas J. Campbell, S. J.

foremost authority on the side of the political theory which he propounded. Cardinal Valerius is quoted as saying of him, "I have scarcely found so many good qualities in a number of excellent men as are combined in this great Christian athlete, in this one great apostle of our age." Cardinal Maphaeus Barbarinus, who later became Pope Urban VIII, regarded Bellarmine as a saint even in his lifetime."[14]

The beatification of Cardinal Bellarmine, May 13th, 1923, by the Congregation of Rites has brought into well deserved present day prominence, this saint and scholar, who to sanctity and learning added a practical interest and activity in the civic and political welfare of his fellowmen.

It is solely, however, as a remarkable political thinker, as a great champion of democracy in the sixteenth and early seventeenth centuries, that Cardinal Bellarmine will engage our attention throughout this treatise. The very principles which the modern world prizes so highly as the foundation of popular and democratic government, and which have procured for millions "life, liberty, and the pursuit of happiness" found their vindication and elucidation in the writings and discourses of this Catholic priest three hundred years ago.

The following chapters will endeavor to show: First, that at a time when the trend towards royal autocracy had grown strong enough for "Divine Right" theorists to proclaim absolute monarchy the best and the solely legitimate form of government, Cardinal Bellarmine contended that the "more useful" form of government is one practically democratic and popular.

Second, when sovereigns began to claim supreme power as a personal prerogative by immediate divine right and appointment, this champion of the popular cause explained how sovereignty is vested in a ruler by the consent of the people.

Third, when the traditional checks imposed upon royal power by constitutional and representative government were being removed, he fought for a continuance of these limitations.

Fourth, when the time honored practice of ecclesiastical limitation of tyranny was being minimized, he proclaimed the spiritual sovereignty of the Church and her relationship to the State.

Fifth, when political rights were being denied, he taught that every state or people has a natural right to determine its own form of government, to resist a tyrannical ruler, and under certain conditions, to depose a ruler.

Sixth, against the practice of some of the more powerful rulers, who preyed upon the territories of smaller nations and spurned ecclesiastical conciliation, he outlined the fundamentals of international law and defined many mutual relations of states in time of peace and war.

---

[14]In an *Epitome and Eulogy of the Life of Robert Cardinal Bellarmine,* written by the Jesuits, Philip Alegamb and Nathanael Sotuellus, and printed at Rome in 1676, the Cardinals Ubaldinus, Centinus, Valerius, and Barbarinus are but four of twelve Cardinals quoted as referring to Cardinal Bellarmine in the highest terms of praise.

Seventh, when civil liberty, human dignity and equality were trampled in the dust, when "passive obedience" and "non-resistance" were unconditionally demanded as the fundamental duty of subjects, he defended popular rights and fearlessly declared subjects as naturally the equals of their rulers, and the office of ruler as merely fiduciary.

Eighth, when kings presumed to claim dictatorship, even over the consciences of men, and attacked their religious liberties, the time honored immunities of clerics and ecclesiastical property, the Cardinal pointed out the novelty and inconsistency of such measures in the light of ancient custom, and of democratic and natural law.

A fuller acquaintance with the political philosophy of this eminent man, whose mind best reveals how the traditional teaching of the Church was applied to the problems of his time, shows that "Democracy" was not the "child of the Reformation," nor the creature of Rousseau and the Encyclopedists or the offspring of revolutionary propaganda or violence.

"The progress of the Constitution, which it was the work of Catholic Ages to build up," says Lord Acton, "was interrupted by the attractions which the growth of absolutism excited and by the Reformation's transferring the ecclesiastical power to the Crown."[15]

The Christian ideal from the beginning, the traditions of the Middle Ages, the great Catholic thinkers and protagonists in the struggle between autocracy and constitutional limitation in the sixteenth and seventeenth centuries,—men like Bellarmine, Suarez—these are the prime sources of true Christian Democracy.

---

[15] *History of Freedom*, p. 208.

CHAPTER I

THE FORM OF POLITICAL GOVERNMENT ADVOCATED BY
CARDINAL BELLARMINE AS THE "MORE USEFUL" WAS, IN
SUBSTANCE, DEMOCRACY.

At the close of the sixteenth century the existence and preponderance of
monarchy was well recognized, but the question to be solved was: Should
royal monarchical power, as the "Divine Right" theorists expounded it,
become absolute—should it so decisively prevail that the other two elements
of recognized government, viz., aristocracy and democracy, be completely
discarded from the political world; or, should a combination of the three,
which had hitherto existed, continue?

Cardinal Bellarmine contended for a continuation of the "combination."
He insisted upon a retention of what we today consider the groundwork of
popular democratic government.

The Cardinal approaches this delicate question of his day with admirable
tact and broad-mindedness. "There are three forms of good government," he
asserts, "monarchy, aristocracy, and democracy." [1]

Without any evidence of prejudice or favoritism he analyzes these three
basic forms and finds that each has its virtues and defects. He then goes on
to demonstrate that an adoption and combination of what is best in each of
these three forms, and a discarding of what is worst, must logically prove to
be a "more useful" form of government.

He weighs monarchy and concludes that, theoretically and in the abstract,
it is indeed the most perfect form of government, for it is employed by the
Creator of the universe; it is in accord with the natural propensity in all
creatures towards a rule by one; it was the government of God's chosen
people in the Old Law, and it is the predominant factor in the constitution of
Christ's Church in the new dispensation.

Hebrew, Greek, and Latin writers of ancient times, theologians,
philosophers, historians, orators, and poets of all ages had recognized in
monarchy a certain dignity and competence which could not be denied. [2]

Monarchy, in the hands of God, Who combines in Himself absolutely all
the qualifications required in an ideal ruler, is indeed a perfect system of
government; in the hands of imperfect man, however, it is exposed to many
defects and abuses. Due to the human element embodied in her, even the
Church, the most perfect society on earth, must supplement many of the
natural limitations of a human monarchy, with a strong admixture of the
aristocratic and the democratic elements.

In the State, a society also of divine origin, but less perfect and less
definite in form, with the human predominantly in the foreground, monarchy
is still more exposed to human excesses and stands in even greater need of
aristocratic and democratic limitation and amplification. "On account of the

---

[1] *De Romani Pontificis Ecclesiastica Monarchia*, Lib. I, Cap. I. 34.

[2] Ibid. Cap. II.

corruption of human nature," the Cardinal says, "we consider as more useful for men at this time a monarchy tempered with aristocracy and democracy rather than simple monarchy."[3] In Bellarmine's time "simple monarchy" meant absolute monarchy, unlimited, unchecked, autocratic power, held by one powerful ruler by divine and incontestable right. Though longing for a strong central power, the masses of the people could not maintain their rights and privileges under so absolute and arbitrary a government. To point out the dangers and defects of absolute monarchy, the Cardinal describes how God refused to grant the Israelites a king,[4] and he concludes; "All these incidents clearly indicate that God did not desire His people to have absolute kings as the Gentiles had them, because He foresaw that they would abuse such power."[5]

Saul, as a private citizen, was a very good man; made king, he became the worst of men, loses his crown and probably his soul. David was so good before he was elevated to the kingship that he would not inflict the slightest injury upon Saul. After he becomes king, he kills one of his trustiest soldiers and pollutes his wife with adultery. Solomon, the wisest of kings at his accession, soon begins to adore idols."[6] Absolute royal power is, therefore, very dangerous in the hands of imperfect man.

Analyzing aristocracy[7] he credits it also with being a good form of government, for it purposes to distribute the various and mainfold duties of

---

[3]Propter naturae humanae corruptionem utiliorem esse censemus hominibus hoc tempore, monarchiam temperatam ex aristocratia et dimocratia. *De Ecclesiastica Monarchia*, Cap I.

[4]I Kings 8: 7-19. "And the Lord said to Samuel: 'Harken to the voice of the people in all that they say to thee.' v, 7...'Now therefore harken to their voice: but yet testify to them.' Then Samuel told all the words of the Lord to the people that had desired a king of him, and said: 'This will be the right of the king, that shall reign over you: He will take your sons, and put them in his chariots, and will make them his horsemen, and his running footmen to run before his chariots, and he will appoint of them to be his tribunes, and centurions, and to plough his fields, and to reap his corn, and to make him arms and chariots. Your daughters also he will take to make him ointments, and to be his cooks, and bakers. And he will take your fields, and your vineyards, and your best oliveyards, and give them to his servants. Moreover he will take the tenth of your corn, and of the revenues of your vineyards, to give his eunuchs and servants. Your servants also and handmaids, and your goodliest young men, and your asses he will take away, and put them to his work. Your flocks also he will tithe, and you shall be his servants. And you shall cry out in that day from the face of the king, whom you have chosen to yourselves: and the Lord will not hear you in that day, because you desired unto yourselves a king.' But the people would not hear the voice of Samuel, and they said: 'Nay: but there shall be a king over us." I Kings. 8: 9-19.

[5] "Haec omnia satis aperte indicant non placuisse Deo, ut populus suus haberet reges absolutos, quomodo habebant gentes." "Deus non probavit regale imperium in populo suo—quia praevidebat Dominus Reges illos male usuros absoluta illa potestate." *De Officio Principis*, Cap. XXII.

[6] *De Officio Principis*, Cap. XXII.

[7] Cf. *De Romano Pontifice* Lib. I. Cap. II, III, IV.

government among the best men of the land. Aristocracy, as applied in the feudal system, had rendered valiant service to society. It had defended Europe against invasion from abroad and against the arrogance of kings at home. It fostered a spirit of true liberty, self-reliance, initiative, and chivalry. On the other hand, aristocracy had its defects. The feuds, dissensions, factions, and disturbances incident to an aristocracy, oligarchy, or plutocracy had proved to be most detrimental to the progress and well-being of that society. Aristocracy led to a division and dissipation of power; it lacked order, harmony and cooperation, strength and endurance.

Democracy too, the Cardinal declares a good form of government, but to proclaim pure and simple democracy as an ideal governmental system would lead to mob violence and the worst form of tyranny; it would precipitate the world into still greater evils. He quotes Plato as saying, "Who can be happy, living under the arbitrary will of a crowd ?"[8]

Each of these simple forms of government had, therefore, been tested in the history of the world before Bellarmine's time and they were found to be wanting. Still there was much in them that was good and useful. Bellarmine would not, therefore, wholly discard any of these systems on account of their defects, but wisely and logically he concludes that a combination of what was best in these simple forms would produce a government possessing the greatest number of desirable qualities conducive to the best interests of men. To be accurate, he does not term this government a monarchy nor an aristocracy nor a democracy, but a "more useful" form of government.[9]

Accordingly, he enumerates the qualities which he considers best in each and which he would incorporate into this more useful form. From the monarchic element he would adopt and embody into this mixed form of government enough to insure order, peace, strength, endurance, and efficiency.

"The first property of good government," he says, " is order. The better the coordination, the better the government. In a monarchy there is no member except the one governing, who is not subject to supreme power. This produces order. Therefore, one finds the greater order in the Catholic Church, in which the faithful are subject to pastors, pastors to their bishops, bishops to the metropolitan, metropolitans to the primate, primates to the Roman Pontiff, the Roman Pontiff to God. In an aristocracy there is order, indeed, in so far as the people are subject to their superiors, but, since the superiors are not subject to any higher unifying power, there is no order among them. Much less can order exist in a simple democracy in which all citizens are of the same condition and authority."[10]

"Another property of good government is peace. Peace is produced and maintained by a union of the members of a state in thought, feeling, and action. But men will be best brought to think, feel, and act alike when they

---

[8] Cf. Ibid. Lib. I. Cap. VI.

[9] Regimen temperatum ex omnibus tribus formis, propter naturae humanae corruptionem utilius est quam simplex monarchia. *De Romani Pontificis Ecclesiastica Monarchia,* Lib I. Cap. III.

[10] *De Romani Pontificis Ecclesiastica Monarchia,* Lib I, Cap. II.

obey, follow, and cling to one ruler, rather than to several. The history of the Romans, e. g., proves this fact; for during the reign of kings or emperors, there were few dissensions, but, under the rule of the magistrates, the patricians were almost constantly in contention with the plebeians. Never did the Roman Empire enjoy greater or more constant peace than under Caesar Augustus, who established the first stable monarchy in Rome."[11]

"A third property of good government is strength and power. The greatest strength and power, however, is developed where there is the greatest and firmest union of members, which, as just noted, is best accomplished in a monarchy. Of the four great empires of the ancient world, three—the Assyrian, the Persian and the Grecian—were monarchies. The Roman State, though developed under popular dominion, was forced to resort to a dictator in the supreme moment of a crisis."[12]

"A fourth property of good government is stability and endurance. Since a monarchy is strongest and most powerful, it is best equipped to withstand external attacks and to avert internal dissolution. It is the least dividing and the most uniting form of organization, while simple aristocracy and democracy are, at most, only an attempt at unity which is seldom attained. Thus the monarchy of the Assyrians from Nino to Sardanapalus endured without interruption some twelve to fourteen hundred years. The kingdom of the Scythians, which is generally regarded as the oldest, lasted several thousand years. The most powerful republic of the Romans numbered scarcely four hundred and eighty years; but under the monarchs of the East, from Julius Caesar to the last Constantine, there was a period of fourteen hundred and ninety-five years. The Republic of Venice continued eleven hundred years, but it was not so old as the Kingdom of the Scythians or of the Assyrians, and, furthermore, it must be noted that it embodied elements of monarchy and aristocracy."[13]

"A fifth property of good government is facility of action and efficiency in the administration. This again is more easily attained in a monarchy. For it is easier to find one good man than many. It is easier to obey one ruler than several. A king who performs the same office constantly learns by experience, while he who rules only for a short while is often removed about the time he has learned to govern. The passing incumbent of an offfice is apt to look to his own emolument, while a more permanent ruler will be inclined to take a continued and personal pride and interest in the realm. When many rule, rivalry, ambition, contention, and a shifting of responsibility arises, which impedes the best functioning of a government. To embody enough of monarchy to insure these good results will, therefore, be most desirable."[14]

Though termed a democracy, our own United States of America bears out the Cardinal's contention. Our federal government with a president as unifying head, our Sovereign states with governors, are monarchic elements

---

[11] *De Rom. Pont. Eccl. Monarchia*, Lib. I, Cap. II.

[12] Ibid.

[13] *De Rom. Pont. Eccl. Monarchia*, Lib. I, Cap. II.

[14] Ibid.

that insure order, peace, and stability.

From the aristocratic type of government the Cardinal would borrow such ideas as seem fitted to supply many of the natural limitations of a one-man rule. Aristocracy, literally, means a rule by the best men of a community. Through such an assisting staff of offficials the various needs and desires of the people may be ascertained and satisfied, at least partially. "With the assistance of the best men of the land the monarch may procure wise counsel. Since it is impossible for one man to superintend all parts of the state and to perform all duties, to have all knowledge, all prudence, all wisdom, all foresight, all counsel and best judgment, a distribution of power," which the Cardinal elsewhere defines as legislative, judicial, and executive,[15] "is most advantageous."[16]

The Cardinal here quotes the incident from Holy Scripture where Moses, upon being reproved by Jethro for attempting to decide all smaller matters himself, "chose able men out of all Israel, and appointed them rulers of the people, rulers over thousands, and over hundreds, and over fifties, and over tens. And they judged the people at all times: and whatsoever was of greater difficulty they referred to him, and they judged the easier causes only."[17]

Rulers like Justinian, for example, became highly efficient and contributed to the well being and progress of society, not so much by their own versatility of mind as by surrounding themselves with a retinue of the ablest men of the land. In our own American Republic, Senators, and Representatives, our Governors of States in relation to the federal government, represent such an "aristocratic" element. According to Cardinal Bellarmine's conception of the "aristocratic" element in government, these governors of provinces and states, or "minor heads," as he calls them, "are not to be regarded as vicars or mere agents of the one supreme head, but in their own territory, they are themselves real and supreme heads. Only in certain general regulations of national import are they subject to higher authority for the sake of unity, order, strength, and cooperation. The minor details of their administration they are to work out themselves according to local conditions and needs. Such a system is calculated to develop greater interest, initiative, originality, and self-expression."[18]

It is interesting to note how often the political ideas of this great Cardinal of three hundred years ago coincide with the Constitution and principles of our own American Government, based on Federal and States' rights.

Thus far Cardinal Bellarmine has combined what is best in monarchy and aristocracy. From the element of democracy he adopts so much, which he fuses into this "more useful" form of government, that his political philosophy presents all those fundamental principles which today are basic in democratic governments. "If the supreme head," he continues, "and the minor heads acquire office not by hereditary succession but by consent of

---

[15] *De Laicis,* Cap. IX to XIII.

[16] *De Rom. Pont. Eccl. Monarchia,* Lib. I, Cap. III.

[17] Exodus 28: 25-26.

[18] *De Ecclesiastica Monarchia,* Cap. III.

the people, then democracy, too, has found its representation in this mixed form of government."[19] The consent of the people he maintains, is necessary in the first instance for a legitimate bestowal of political authority upon any particular ruler.[20] An appeal or referendum to the people is also possible.[21] The laws proposed by the magistrate receive their binding force from the people.[22]

The community has a right not only to elect their rulers, but also to determine and change the system of government, to limit and, in extreme cases, to depose a tyrannical ruler.[23] "Such a mixed and more useful government" he concludes, "would therefore first, embrace one supreme head and possess all the good qualities attributed to monarchy: order, peace, power, stability, efficiency, second; provide such minor heads as governors of provinces, legislators, and judges who, on the one hand, would be in harmony with the supreme head and assist in distributing the burdens of government, and on the other hand, be independent enough to govern over their provinces, not as the property of another, but as their own, thus making the best qualities of an aristocracy also possible; third, contain such democratic elements as should reasonably insure the Commonwealth against incompetent rulers and secure the highest degree of popular right, liberty, approval, self-expression, participation, and welfare."[24]

The necessary conclusion of this chapter is that, while Divine Right theorists were extolling absolute monarchy and discarding every trace of aristocratic and democratic government, Cardinal Bellarmine outlined and defended a form of government which, in a strict sense, was neither monarchy nor aristocracy nor democracy, but which contained the fundamental principles, the embryo and potentiality of giving to the world a theory of state that was truly democratic and most useful.

Etymologically analyzed, democracy indicates a rule by the people, of the people, and for the people. While government by the people enters into the definition, government for the people is the touchstone of real democracy. The best type of government is that which best serves the greatest number of men; which distributes the opportunities and goods of the earth as justly and equitably as the varying needs and capacities of men dictate; which stimulates the latent energy and resources of individual personality; which maintains order, peace, happiness and liberty at home and by its inherent efficiency, strength, endurance and power, inspires respect abroad; a government, finally, which lays no obstacles in the way of man's eternal

---

[19] *De Eccl. Mon.* Cap. III.

[20] *De Laicis,* Cap. VI; *De Eccl. Mon.* Ch. VI.

[21] *De Eccl. Mon* Cap. VI. "Ubi est populare regimen, appellatur a sententia magistratus in rebus gravioribus ad judicium populi."

[22] Ibid. Cap. VI. "Leges quibus Respublica gubernanda est. a magistratu quidem proponuntur, sed a populo jubentur."

[23] *De Rom. Pont. Eccl. Monarchia,* Lib. I, Cap. VI. Nota quarta. *De Laicis,* Cap. VI; also *Recognitio, Libri Tertii De Laicis.*

[24] *De Eccl. Mon.* Cap. III.

destiny. Call that government what you will, democracy seems best to express its character. Such was the ideal of good government proposed and defended by this illustrious Cardinal of the Church, at a time when absolute monarchy was clamoring to be the best, the sole legitimate form of government.

CHAPTER II
HIS THEORY OF POPULAR SOVEREIGNTY

It is universally conceded by historians that in mediaeval political theory, the authority of a civil ruler was generally founded in the election or recognition of the community. Otto Gierke states, "An ancient and generally entertained opinion regarded the will of the people as the source of temporal power; political authority by divine grant and absolute power was wholly foreign to the Middle Ages."[1]

James Bryce, in referring to the "Defensor Pacis," by Marsilius of Padua, as "one of the most remarkable treatises that remains to us from the Middle Ages," says, "In holding that the ultimate source of power is in the people, Marsilius does not stand alone, for this position is to be found in other mediaeval publicists."[2] Dr. A. J. Carlyle asserts, "The Emperor derived his authority, ultimately no doubt, from God, but immediately from the nation,"[3] and this fact, he adds, "requires no serious demonstration."[4]

As already noted, a tendency towards absolute autocracy was manifesting itself for some time among the more powerful rulers of Western Europe even before the Reformation. All acknowledged that the spiritual sovereignty of the Pope was of divine origin and direct appointment and that in virtue thereof, he, as the acknowledged guardian of the faithful, might intervene, for spiritual reasons, in matters of state.

Some were of the opinion that all power, even the temporal, was derived from God through the Pontiff. Kings and emperors therefore, who came into conflict with the ecclesiastical authorities began to devise counter theories which placed the title of civil authority, in the same manner as that of the ecclesiastical, in an immediate and direct divine appointment. In this manner they hoped to assert their superior claims with a semblance of justification. Their theory was later known as the "Divine Right of Kings."

The religious revolt against Rome in the first half of the sixteenth century gave new impetus to the rapid expansion of this absolutist tendency. "Royal power must be exalted as against that of the Pope," was the cry of the divine right theorists. "Luther based royal authority upon divine right with practically no reservation."[5] "Calvin judged that the people are unfit to govern themselves and declared the popular assembly an abuse."[6] Bluntchli remarks that "after the Reformation the Lutheran theologians began to proclaim the saying of Paul, 'the powers that be, are ordained of God,' as a Christian dogma and to declare those in authority the anointed representatives of God. They did not consider that the Apostle Paul

---

[1] Gierke, *Political Theories of the Middle Ages*, p. 38-39.

[2] James Bryce, *The Holy Roman Empire*, p. 225.

[3] *History of Mediaeval Political Theory in the West*, Vol. I, p. 292.

[4] Ibid. Vol. III, p. 153.

[5] Figgis, *Gerson to Grotius*, p. 61.

[6] Lord Acton, *History of Freedom*, p. 42.

expressly applied that saying to the Roman Emperor Nero, who had received his power from the Roman people and meant to oppose the theocratically minded Jewish Christians who condemned the heathen emperor."[7] "Lutheran writers constantly condemned the democratic literature that arose in the second age of the Reformation."[8]

That the establishment of such a theory was destructive of popular rights as well as of papal claims was not generally realized at first. "That these positions were destructive of popular rights is not yet seen," says Figgis; "monarchy will be defended for its own sake when Bellarmine and Suarez have elaborated their theory of popular sovereignty."[9]

The value of any theory or doctrine is best tried in the purging fires of opposition. It is then that a worthwhile principle will attract to its defense the ablest minds. Foremost among those to whom fell the task of vindicating and expounding the traditional doctrine of popular sovereignty against the new teachings of absolute divine right, was the illustrious and now Blessed Cardinal Bellarmine. It need not be denied that the Cardinal, in controverting the divine right theorists, aimed at the defense of the Church as well as the defense of the people, since absolute monarchy, by divine right, was inimical to the interests of Church and people alike.

The theory of Divine Right was, in its general characteristics, the following: The king derives his power immediately and directly from God. The king has a hereditary and a divine right to rule. The duty of the king is to govern like a father; the duty of a subject is to obey like a child. "The king can do no wrong" was the dictum of Robert Filmer in his Patriarcha. If the king does wrong, is cruel, unjust, and governs badly, the people are indeed unfortunate but under no circumstances have they any recourse except by prayer to God. The king is accountable to God alone. "The most sacred order of kings is of Divine Right."[10] Sovereignty is a property of the king, not of the state.

This theory was supported by Scriptural references like the following: "Render to Caesar the things that are Cesar's";[11] "There is no power but from God: and those that are, are ordained of God";[12] "By Me kings reign, and lawgivers decree just things";[13] "Honor the kings,"[14] and similar texts.

The outstanding features of the theory of the Divine Right of Kings at the close of the sixteenth century were, according to John Neville Figgis, the following: First, monarchy is a divinely ordained institution. Second, hereditary right is indefeasible. The right acquired by birth cannot be

---

[7] Bluntschli, *Theory of State,* p. 291.

[8] Lord Acton, *History of Freedom,* p. 42.

[9] *Divine Right of Kings,* p. 92.

[10] *Constitutions and Canons of the Church of England.*

[11] Luke 20:25.

[12] Romans 13:1-7.

[13] Proverbs 8:15.

[14] I St. Peter: 2:17.

forfeited through any acts of usurpation, of however long continuance, by any incapacity in the heir, or by any act of deposition. So long as the heir lives, he is king by hereditary right, even though the usurping dynasty has reigned for a thousand years. Third, kings are accountable to God alone. Sovereignty is vested in the king whose power has no legal limitation. All law is mere concession of his will, and all constitutional form and assemblies exist entirely at his pleasure. Fourth, non-resistance and passive obedience are enjoined by God. Whenever the king issues a command directly contrary to God's law, God is to be obeyed rather than man, but the penalties attached to the breach of the law are to be patiently endured." [15]

In contrast to the above, it may be well first, to state as briefly as possible the mediaeval traditional view as expounded by Cardinal Bellarmine and then to investigate his theory more in detail. In substance it is this: The nation is an organic group, a political unit, composed of individuals. Each individual is by nature born free and equal. Being free and equal, there is no reason why one man should have a greater right to rule than another; still, society is of such a nature that inherently it needs a ruler for its common welfare and self-preservation.

The right, then, to some kind of good government, the necessity of a sovereign power, flows from the very nature of society; it is an attribute of society, a prerogative of the state; it is, therefore of divine origin; it does not depend upon the consent or compact or contract of any individual in that society. Who in particular from among these equals shall be vested with this power, which form of government shall be the accepted one—this the nature and constitution of society does not define; this is a matter which is to be determined by the will of the people as a political body.

In the first place, then, Cardinal Bellarmine proves that temporal power, or political authority in general, is necessary and good and that it is primarily of divine origin. So far he agrees with the Divine Right theorists. "It is certain," he says, "that political authority comes from God." [16] Indeed the Wisdom of God cries aloud, 'By Me kings reign.—By Me princes rule.' [17] 'The most High ruleth over the kingdom of men and giveth it to whomsoever he will." [18]

After proving by the Sacred Scriptures that all civil authority comes from God, he presents his theory as to how these Scriptural statements are to be interpreted. "First," he says, "it is to be observed that political power, considered in general, and without entering into the question of monarchy, aristocracy, or democracy, proceeds from God alone; for it is necessarily annexed to human nature and emanates from Him who made that nature. Moreover, this power exists by the natural law, since it does not depend upon the consent of man; for whether they will or not they must be governed

---

[15] *Divine Right of Kings,* p. 5.

[16] *De Laicis,* Cap. VI.

[17] Proverbs 8:15-16.

[18] Daniel 4:22. Cf. Daniel 2:37.

by someone lest they be willing to perish, which is not human."[19] "It is impossible for many to exist together without someone to care for the public good. Society is a multitude with order, not a crowd with confusion. Order is but a series of inferiors and superiors. Therefore, leaders are necessary if society would thrive."[20] "It is thus that the law of nature is a divine law and by divine law, therefore, government has been introduced into the world.[21] This is what St. Paul really wished to express when he said, "He that resisteth the power, resisteth the ordinance of God."[22]

So far, the Cardinal has laid down a doctrine which no Christian dares deny. Any contrary theory would rob the civil authority of every higher origin and sanction. The principle of Rousseau,[23] Hobbes,[24] Locke,[25] and Pufendorf,[26] that sovereignty is created in the first instance by the contribution of each individual's presumed sovereignty by "social compact," is erroneous, absurd in theory, unhistorical, and politically dangerous; for, if any individual refused to yield his share of sovereignty and independence, government would become entirely impossible. Indissolubly connected with the name of Rousseau is the theory which assumes but does not prove individuals as making contracts—contracts giving judicial existence to a

---

[19] *De Laicis,* Cap. VI.

[20] Ibid. Cap. V.

[21] Hic observanda sunt aliqua. Primo, politicam potestatem in universum consideratam, non descendendo in particulari ad monarchiam, aristocratiam, vel dimocratiam, immediate esse a solo Deo: nam consequitur necessario naturam hominis, proinde esse ab illo, qui fecit naturam hominis. Praeterea haec potestas est de jure naturae, non enim pendet ex consensu hominum; nam velint, nolint, debent regi ab aliquo, nisi velint perire humanum genus, quod est contra naturae inclinationem. At jus naturae est jus divinum, jure igitur divino introducta est gubernatio. *De Laicis,* Ch. VI, note I.

[22] Romans 13:2.

[23] "Trouver une forme d' association qui defende et protege de toute la force commune la personne et les biens de chaque associe, et par laquelle chacun, s'unissant a tous, n'obeisse pourtant qu' a, lui-meme et reste aussi libre qu auparavant: tel est le problem fondamental dont le contrat social."—Rousseau, *Contrat social*, I, Ch. 6.

[24] Civitas ergo est persona una, cuius voluntas ex pactis plurium hominum pro voluntate habenda est ipsorum hominum." Hobbes, *De Cive,* C 5. par. 9. Molesworth's Edit. Vol. II, p. 214. "Men pass from the state of nature to the social state by surrendering their rights to a sovereign" (one or many). Hobbes, *Leviathan* Ch. 17.

[25] Locke's *Treatises on Government,* Book 2, Ch. VIII, 97, suppose rights to exist in the state of nature, and by "original compact" (not contract) a form of government is instituted to secure these rights. "When any number of men have by the consent of every individual, made a community, they have thereby made that community one body."

[26] Unde civitatis haec commodissima videtur definitio, quod sit persona moralis composita, cuius voluntas ex plurium pactis implicita et unita pro voluntate omnium habetur, ut singulorum viribus et facultatibus ad pacem et securitatem communem uti possit." Pufendorf, "De jure naturali et gentium, VII, 2, 13.

body politic.

If individuals make contracts, private rights are created, but not public rights. A contract, if political, does not deal with the private good of individuals, but with the public good of the community. Thus neither a nation nor a state can arise out of contract between individuals. A sum of individual wills does not produce a common will any more than a number of apples produce a sum of pears.

The renunciation of any number of private rights does not produce any public right. In the Middle Ages "the powers ascribed to the community of the people were not the private rights of a sum of individuals but the public right of a constitutionally compounded assembly." [27]

History does not afford a single instance in which a state has really been formed by contract or compact between individuals. For practical politics this theory is in the highest degree dangerous, since it exposes the state and its institutions to the caprice of individuals. In fact this theory was one contributing cause of the French Revolution. According to Bellarmine, civil society is the natural condition into which every individual is born as "a social animal." [28]

Society does not derive its authority from any social contract or agreement, tacit or expressed, as Althusius, for instance, or Grotius, Hooker, Hobbes, Locke, Rousseau, Puffendorf, Kant, Fichte, with slight variation of doctrine, maintained. Government includes powers which never belonged to the individual and which, consequently, he could never have conferred upon society.

The individual surrenders no authority; sovereignty receives nothing from him. According to our exponent, government maintains its full dignity; it is of divine origin; "there is no power but from God, and those that are, are ordained of God." [29]

"Whether a people transfers its power to a ruler, or whether the ruler acquires power by hereditary succession or by the right of war, no matter by what title, it will always remain true that his power comes from God." [30] Hence it is obvious how far removed the thought of Bellarmine was from that of political reformers like Rousseau, Hobbes, Locke, and others.

The next step in Bellarmine's theory explains with whom God, in the first instance, has deposited this supreme power. "Political power," he continues, "resides immediately in the whole multitude as in an organic unit. The divine law has not given this power to any particular man; therefore, it has given it to the multitude."

There being no positive law to this effect, there is no more reason why, among equals, one should have a greater right to rule than another. Therefore, the power belongs to the whole multitude. Sovereignty and public rights arise not from the combined contribution of private rights, but from

---

[27] Gierke, *Political Theories of the Middle Ages,* p. 63.

[28] *De Laicis,* Cap. V.

[29] Romans 13:1.

[30] *De Officio Principis,* Cap. I.

the public or social right which lies in the multitude, and not in the individual. Finally, human society ought to be a perfect state; if so, then it should have the faculties to preserve itself and to punish disturbers of the peace."[31]

The conclusion is: The natural or divine law, which creates political power in general, creates and vests it immediately and directly, not in any individual, not in any king, but in the multitude, the community, thought of as a political unit. Here he departs from a Divine Right theory of kings, which insisted that God placed this authority immediately in the person of some particular royal personage.

The next question that presents itself is: How shall society or the "multitude" use this power? "The community," he says, "being unable to exercise this power itself, is obliged to communicate it to one or to several. In this manner, the power of princes considered in general, is, indeed, by natural and divine law; and the whole human race if assembled could not establish the contrary."[32]

But, that this or that particular person rule, is determined by the choice of society. "Particular forms of government are also determined by the law of nations, not by the divine law, for it depends upon the consent of the multitude to place over themselves a king, consul, or other magistrate; and if there be a legitimate reason, the multitude can change the government into an aristocracy or a democracy, or vice versa, as was done in Rome."[33] The political power which is concretely vested in any particular ruler, he explains, comes, indeed, from God originally, but by means of a deliberation and election of men—by the law of nations, which is a reasoned conclusion

---

[31] Secundo nota, hanc potestatem immediate esse tamquam in subjecto, in tota multitudine: nam haec potestas est de jure divino. At jus divinum nulli homini particulari dedit hanc potestatem: ergo dedit multitudini. Praeterea sublato jure positivo, non est major ratio cur ex multis aequalibus unus potius, quam alius dominetur. Igitur potestas totius est multitudinis. Denique humana societas debet esse perfecta respublica: ergo debet habere potestatem seipsam conservandi, et proinde puniendi perturbatores pacis. *De Laicis,* Cap. VI.

[32] Tertio nota, hanc potestatem transferri a multitudine in unum vel plures eodem jure naturae: nam respublica non potest per se ipsam exercere hanc potestatem: ergo tenetur eam transferre in aliquem unum, vel aliquos paucos, et hoc modo potestas principum in genere considerata, est etiam de jure naturae et divino, nec posset genus humanum, etiamsi totum simul conveniret, contrarium statuere nimirum, ut nulli essent principes vel rectores. *De Laicis,* Cap. V.

[33] Quarto nota, in particulari singulas species regiminis esse de jure gentium, non de jure naturae, nam pendet a consensu multitudinis, constituere super se regem vel consules, vel alios magistratus, ut patet: et si causa legitima adsit, potest multitudo mutare regnum in aristocratiam aut dimocratiam, et a contrario, ut Romae factum legimus. *De Laicis,* Ch. VI.

drawn from the natural law." [34]

He corroborates his arguments by several examples from Holy Scripture. The words of Samuel to Saul, "Behold, the Lord hath anointed thee to be prince over his inheritance," [35] Bellarmine interprets as a proclamation rather than as a transfer of power. For, a little later, Samuel calls the people together for the purpose of selecting a king, and the lot falls upon Saul. But, because not a few refused to acquiesce in the election, Samuel, in the next chapter, 11: 14-15, says to the people, "Come let us go to Galgal, and let us renew the Kingdom there...And all the people went to Galgal and there they made Saul King before the Lord in Galgal—and there Saul and all the men of Israel rejoiced exceedingly." Bellarmine then argues that "God, indeed, designated Saul as King and by His Providence arranged that the lot fell to him and again later inclined the will of the people to desire him as King. Therefore, not without the consent of the people nor immediately by God, was Saul made King." [36]

The anointing of David by Samuel [37] Bellarmine also pronounces a mere proclamation, not a transfer of power. This is plain from the fact that David, after his anointment still recognized and honored Saul as the king, as long as he lived; nor did he dare assume royal authority at the death of Saul, until such authority was conferred on him by the people. [38] Bellarmine again concludes, "God, indeed, made David a king, as he had promised, but by means of the consent of the people. Likewise, God elected Jeroboam king [39] but he finished the appointment " [40] by consent of the people, who rebelled against Roboam and constituted Jeroboam king. If, therefore, those whom God himself designates and makes king, He does not so make without the consent of the people, certainly other rulers chosen in other ways, cannot be said to receive their political power immediately from God." [41]

The most vehement opponent of Cardinal Bellarmine during his lifetime was undoubtedly King James I, who ascended the English throne in 1603. In

---

[34] Quinto nota, ex dictis sequi, hanc potestatem in particulari esse quidem a Deo, sed mediante consilio et electione humana, ut alia omnia quae ad jus gentium pertinent. Jus enim gentium est quasi conclusio deducta ex jure naturae per humanum discursum. *De Laicis,* Cap. VI.

[35] I Kings 10:1.

[36] *Recognito Libri tertii, De Laicis.*

[37] I Kings 16: 13.

[38] And the men of Juda came and anointed David, to be King over the house of Juda." II Kings 2:4.

"Then all the tribes of Israel came to David in Hebron, saying 'we are thy bone and thy flesh—thou shalt be prince over Israel.' The ancients also of Israel came—and they anointed David to be King over Israel." II Kings 5: 1-3.

[39] III Kings 11:37.

[40] III Kings 12:20.

[41] *Recognitio Libri Tertii, De Laicis.*

his "Triplici Nodo"[42] he bitterly arraigned Bellarmine for saying that Saul, David, and Jeroboam, although anointed kings by the prophets, did not begin to reign without the consent of the people. "He (Bellarmine) hath made the people and the subjects of every one of us our superiors." To this complaint of James, Bellarmine replied, "The authority of the king descends, not immediately from God nor by divine right, but only by the law of nations. This has been indeed, the common opinion of almost all writers and the general usage and practice of the past.

"We see, for instance, how kingdoms have been converted into republics and republics into kingdoms, and both rules were regarded as equally just. This could not be so if the authority of kings did not depend on the common consent, but on divine right."[43]

Shortly after the retort of James, William Barclay, a Catholic jurist of Angers in France, attacked the theory of Bellarmine. He claimed that rulers have their authority from God in the sense that they are under God alone, and that only God can deprive them of their power. In response, Bellarmine repeats his original doctrine that "all power is indeed from God, but some power is immediately from God, as that of Moses or of St. Peter, or of St. Paul, and other power comes mediately by the consent of the people, as the power of kings, consuls and tribunes, for as St. Thomas says,"[44] 'human dominions and princedoms are by human right, not by divine right.'"[45]

From the preceding arguments and discussions we gather unmistakably that Bellarmine insisted absolutely upon the consent of the people as the immediate source of particular sovereign power. "The original sovereignty of the people." says Figgis, "is a cardinal doctrine of Jesuit thinkers."[46]

In connection with this point it may be interesting to note the Cardinal's view on election, which is in strict accordance with the foregoing theory of popular sovereignty.

As a general principle, he assumes that the election of a ruler, political or ecclesiastical, is in most cases better than hereditary succession. He points to the example of the Church, which, being the most perfect society founded by God, receives its ministers, not by heredity, which the very law of celibacy precludes, but by choice and deliberation."[47]

In his admonition to kings he makes the statement that "in an election, reason, age, knowledge, prudence, and the best moral qualifications are considered in the choice. Kings often succeed their fathers, and it is not rare that unworthy sons follow worthy fathers; a foolish son, a prudent father."[48] From mediaeval history he draws the argument that rulers chosen by the people or their representatives were always regarded as possessing equally

---

[42] p. 124.

[43] Bellarmine, *Apologia Pro Juramento Fidelitatis.*

[44] St. Thomas, 2. 2 ques. 10, art. 10 et quest. 12, art. 2.

[45] Bellarmine, *De Potestate Papae in Rebus Temporalibus,* Cap. III, obj. 10.

[46] *Gerson to Grotius,* p. 155.

[47] Cf. *De Clericis,* Cap. VI.

[48] *De Officio Principis Christiani,* Cap. XXII.

as good a title as they who reigned by some law of heredity.[49]

Conrad (911-918), last of the Carolingian Emperors, was elected by all the people of the Franks and Saxons. Henry I, Conrad's successor (919-936), and the three Ottos (936-1002) were elected. Again, by the election of Lothar (1125) the Swabian family was ousted from what it had come to regard almost as an hereditary possession.

The Cardinal also cites the case of Albert who contended with Pope Boniface VIII to assure his heirs a hereditary right to the throne; but Boniface insisted that the emperor "should be elected, not born."

He does not consider other titles to political authority as invalid, so long as they rest on the consent of the people."[50]

"Men endowed with human reason," he says, "are born free and cannot be subjected one to another except by just title, such as election, succession, or others known to all."[51]

A brief review of the chapter shows that Cardinal Bellarmine thus far vindicated in unmistakable terms the following points:

(1) All power is originally derived from God.

(2) Political power is good and necessary; it does not depend upon the compact, agreement, or consent of any one; but it was instituted by God concomitantly with the foundation of society.

(3) The immediate title to sovereign power lies in the consent of the people as a political body.

(4) The particular form of government to be employed is determined by the consent of the people or by the law of nations, not by the law of nature.

(5) Election is the most prudent and satisfactory manner of selecting a sovereign and the government's personnel.

These principles were fundamental in the generally accepted political doctrine of mediaeval times; they are still the groundwork of any well balanced and refined democracy today.

---

[49] *Recognitio Libri Tertii De Laicis.*

[50] Bellarmine, *De Translatione,* Cap. VII.

[51] *De Officio Principis Christiani,* Cap. XXII.

CHAPTER III
CONSTITUTIONAL LIMITATION

Another mediaeval tradition, which the divine right theorists and monarchs were discarding in the days of Cardinal Bellarmine, was representative government and constitutional limitation of royal power.

It is universally admitted that the Middle Ages had developed a rather complete system of constitutional government. "Constitutional limitation was a mediaeval tradition," [1] says Carlton J. H. Hayes.

"Looking back over the space of a thousand years," remarks Lord Acton, "which we call the Middle Ages, to get an estimate of the work they had done, we find that representative government was almost universal. Absolute power was deemed more intolerable and more criminal than slavery." [2]

"Mediaeval doctrine," according to Otto Gierke, "gave to the monarch a representative character" [3]

In Spain the Council of Toledo (587) furnished the framework of a parliamentary system, perhaps the oldest in the world. Then followed the period of feudalism, in which monarchy was well limited by a strong aristocracy.

"The king had no legislative power by himself. The counsel and consent of the national estates were necessary for the edicts of the king; the approval of the provincial estates, for those of the prince." [4]

In England the beginnings of parliament are traced back to a period even prior to the Norman Conquest, in 1066. The Magna Charta, of 1215, safeguarded English liberty against King John I and clearly defined the ancient rights and privileges of prince and people.

In 1265 the House of Commons was formed as another factor in upholding constitutional freedom. Some of the powers and duties of parliament were to inform and to advise the king, to grant or refuse subsidies, to sanction the levying of taxes, to secure royal enactment of laws, to demand an account of expenditures.

The revolution of 1399 in England against Richard II was another assertion of the rights of Englishmen to constitutional government. The articles of deposition against Richard formed a complete system of

---

[1] *Political and Social History of Modern Europe*, Vol. I, p. 264.

[2] *History of Freedom*, p. 39.

[3] *Political Theories of the Middle Ages*, p. 61.

[4] Bluntschli, *Theory of State*, p. 388.

constitutional limitation.[5]

Parliament asserted its right to elect the fittest person when it elevated to the throne Henry of Bolingbroke in place of the nearest heir. "The rules and forms of parliamentary procedure had, before the close of the Middle Ages, begun to acquire that permanence and fixedness of character which in the eyes of later generations, had risen into the sanctity of law."[6]

A turning point in the history of constitutional government came with the Renaissance and the Reformation. The spirit of the Renaissance revived the pagan ideas of Caesarism. Since the fifteenth century potentates began to trample under foot the rights of people and Church.

The revolt against the papacy in the sixteenth century enlarged the powers of princes, and they claimed the right to regulate even the consciences of their subjects.

"The Renaissance weakened the mediaeval constitution and the Reformation overthrew it."[7] "The Reformation had left upon the statute book an emphatic assertion of unfettered sovereignty vested in the king."[8]

In Germany, "Luther denied any limitation of political power either by Pope or people; nor can it be said that he showed any sympathy for representative institutions; he upheld the inalienable and divine authority of kings in order to hew down the Upas tree of Rome."[9]

In England the Tudor kings since Henry VII made themselves more and more independent of parliamentary grants by an economic conduct of government.

With the accession of James I (1603), however, who needed extensive parliamentary subsidies to carry out his extravagant plans, the struggle between king and parliament was renewed.

In France constitutional limitation was similarly yielding to royal autocracy. Its early advocate was Philip the Fair. Since the accession of Louis XI in 1461, the Estates General had not been convened until 1614. Only for the short period of three weeks was it convened in 1614 under Marie de'Medici.

"How did the sixteenth century," asks Lord Acton, "husband the treasure

---

[5] Shakespeare depicting the fickle character of Richard II represents him as proclaiming divine right of kings in language such as would have delighted James I. "Not all the water in the rough rude sea can wash the balm off from an anointed king; the breath of worldly men cannot depose the deputy elected by the Lord." (Richard II. Act, iii, Scene 2.) Shakespeare does not correctly record the historical fact, however, when after the deposition he quotes Richard as saying: Act. iv, Scene 1. "With mine own tears I wash away my balm, With mine own hands I give away my crown, With mine own tongue deny my sacred state, With mine own breath release all duty's rites." For Parliament forced him to renounce all honors and dignities pertaining to a king.

[6] Stubbs, *Constitutional History of England*, Vol. III, p. 388.

[7] DeVos, *Fifteen Hundred Years of Europe*, p. 42.

[8] Figgis, *Divine Right of Kings*, p. 91.

[9] Figgis, *Cambridge Modern History*, Vol. III, p. 739.

which the Middle Ages had stored up?"[10] Figgis gives the answer: "There had been elaborated at this time a theory of unlimited jurisdiction of the crown and of non-resistance upon any pretense."[11] Unlimited monarchy was establishing itself in Europe, especially in England, as a divine institution. The ancient and once universally accepted theory and practice of constitutional limitation, election, and popular rights, all seemed forever relegated to the past.

Against this tendency the whole political doctrine of Cardinal Bellarmine revolted. "In temporal governments," he contended, "supreme power resides in the king, but this power is derived from the people and is radically in, and supplied by the kingdom. The people make the king, who otherwise would be a private individual like the rest of men, naturally free and equal. Nor can one man command all others unless they subject themselves to him and concede to him power over themselves."[12]

His contention that civil authority was constituted by popular consent involved another great democratic principle, viz., the right of the community to limit and qualify the exercise of sovereign power. If the community has a right, was in substance his argument, to confer the whole of political power upon any particular individual, why has it not a right also to that which is less, viz., to place conditions under which this transfer is to take place? If the community has in itself the right to limit its appointee in the exercise of the powers conferred, why has it not also the right to determine the method and-means of limitation?

In other words, it may constitute such representative bodies, variously known as parliaments, national assemblies, or congresses, to partake in the government of the realm. "When a controversy arises in the republic," he says, "the princes and magistrates of the realm come together and determine what action should be taken."[13]

"Since one man cannot attend to all matters of state, he must distribute these powers. While it is evident that monarchy contains necessary features of government, yet all love that form of government best in which they can participate. Of the utility of such a government we need scarcely speak, since it is certain that no one man can himself govern many provinces and states.

"The Jewish people always had one judge or leader or king but it also had many minor princes, as we read in the book of Exodus."[14] The plea of Cardinal Bellarmine as presented in chapter I of this treatise, for an embodiment of certain features of aristocratic government, harmonizes with the present argument.

From mediaeval history he draws numerous examples in proof of the

---

[10] Lord Acton, *History of Freedom*, p. 40.

[11] Figgis, *Cambridge Modern History*, Vol. III, p. 740.

[12] Bellarmine, *De Conciliorum Auctoritate,* Cap. XVI.

[13] Bellarmine, *De Conciliis et Ecclesia*, Cap. III.

[14] *De Romani Pontificis Ecclesiastica Monarchia*, Ch. III.

limitation of kings in many ways. He relates, for instance, that Charles the Great made a will by which he distributed the empire among his sons. This will was not considered valid until signed by the nobles and approved and subscribed to by the Pope.[15]

He quotes Innocent III as saying to the Duke of Thuringia, "We recognize that those princes have the right and power to elect a king, afterwards to be approved by the emperor, who by law and custom are known to have such power."[16]

Another phase of constitutional limitation was the restriction which the law of the land might place upon the sovereign will. Dr. A. J. Carlyle states, "It is hardly necessary to multiply citations to establish a judgment which is almost universally accepted as to the constitutional theory .... that the king does not make laws by his own authority but requires the consent and advice of his wise men, and, in some more or less vague sense, of the whole nation.[17]

Towards the close of the sixteenth century considerable controversy centered around the origin and sphere of the law. Cardinal Bellarmine quotes Calvin as maintaining that it is the duty of the Church to make civil laws, to institute courts, and to use the sword; otherwise civil laws could have no binding force in conscience. John Gerson and Almain before Calvin taught the same. Some of their reasons for this contention were: "The political power, being temporal, has nothing to do with conscience; the prince, unable to inflict spiritual punishment, is unable to obligate in conscience; since the prince cannot absolve, he cannot bind nor can he intend to bind in conscience."[18]

Supporters of divine right went to the opposite extreme and were constantly contending that there could be no permanent uniform, universal law or constitution, independent of the lawgiver; that the king was the whole source of law; that the ruler's will was the *lex animata*, the animated law; and that the king himself was not bound by the law. *What pleases the prince has the vigor of law, the prince is free from the law*, were adopted as axioms of divine right theory. "Wycliffe would not allow that the king is subject to positive law."[19]

William Barclay contended that kings are above all human and positive laws; that they give an account to God alone; that there can be no indictment against the king, since he is safe in the power of his throne; that although he fails against the law, he is not bound by it. "If kings are not bound by the law," Bellarmine responded, "how can they fail against the law? Where there

---

[15] Cf. *De Translatione Romani Imperii*, Ch. V.

[16] Ibid.

[17] *History of Mediaeval Political Theory in the West*, Vol. I, p. 238.

[18] *De Laicis*, Cap. IX.

[19] Figgis, *Divine Right of Kings*, p. 69.

is no law there is no transgression."[20] James I summarized his idea upon this point in the famous epigram, "*A Deo rex, a rege lex*"—"The king is from God, the law from the king."

Against both extremes Bellarmine set up the proposition that "it is lawful for rulers to frame laws, that civil laws, although less firm and stable, bind no less in conscience than divine laws; that kings, too, are bound by the law."

"The power of obligating," he says, "is of the essence of every natural law, human or divine. Just laws cannot be made except by one having authority, and no one has such authority but ultimately from God.

"Every just law, then, founded by legitimate authority is a participation of the eternal law, which always binds in conscience. A just civil law is always a conclusion or determination of the divine moral law, with this difference, that the human law has in mind external acts of charity, such as peace and the conservation of the republic; the divine law looks to the spiritual and internal acts of charity. Therefore both have the same purpose."[21]

The champions of popular sovereignty insisted that the force of statute law always had its source primarily in the consent of the community, that the power of the state stood below the rules of natural and above the rules of positive law, that law was the practical form of justice, that maintenance of the law secured every good in life.

With St. Thomas they defined law as "the constant and perpetual will which concedes to every man his right; and at the bottom of the law they found love, charity. Reason is a participation of the eternal law of God; human law is a participation of reason; if the law and decrees of princes violate reason, they are unjust and not binding."[22]

"Unjust laws are, properly speaking, no laws," says Bellarmine, and he teaches with St. Augustine that four conditions are necessary in order that a law may be just.

"First, the law must be conducive to public welfare. As a king differs from a tyrant in this, that the king seeks the common good, while the tyrant seeks his own good, so a just law differs from a tyrannical law.

"Second, the law must be made and imposed by one properly constituted in authority.

"Third, the law must not prohibit virtue nor encourage vice. Fourth, the law must be constituted and promulgated in official form and order. It must observe a right and just apportionment of honors and burdens in the republic."[23]

"A bad law is not a valid law," says Bellarmine. "Good laws are not a curtailment of liberty, but the charter of every man's right.

"When laws do not protect men's rights, but infringe upon them, when laws are an impediment to the community's development and welfare, they

---

[20] *De Potestate Papae in Rebus Temp.*, contra Barclaium, Cap. XXII.

[21] *De Laicis*, Cap. XI.

[22] St. Thomas, *Summa Theologica*, 2a, 2ae, ques. LVIII. a. i.

[23] *De Romano Pontifice*, Lib. IV, Caput XV.

not good laws and they are therefore not valid laws."[24]

He by no means, however, belittles the sovereign's dignity and power once committed to him. In the ninth chapter of "De Laicis" he clearly states, "It is lawful for the magistrate to make laws, to exercise justice, to punish crimes, for so the Scriptures define, 'by me kings reign and law-givers decree just things, by me princes rule and the mighty decree justice.'"[25]

Civil laws are necessary to regulate the commercial and social relations of life, since the natural law and general principles do not descend to such details. Neither does the evangelical law sufficiently touch upon such temporal matters." [26]

The decisions and commands of the king, he maintains, may not always be adequate, and a people may have need to be ruled by permanently constituted laws rather than by the immediate will of the ruler. He admits that one might find exceptional cases where the rule of a wise regent over a small group of people might prove sufficient; he admits that people have been ruled without such laws, as, for instance, the Roman republic; but he continues: "If a people be ruled by the judgment of a king, it will be necessary to have the very best kind of kings at all times; if it be ruled by laws, however, it will suffice that at one time, at least, there were wise and good regents. Good laws, once made, remain; a good king will die.

Laws are generally the combined judgment and experience of several wise men; the king's command is the judgment of one man, and it may be rash. Legislators are less exposed to favoritism or bias; a ruler may be influenced by friends, relatives, bribes, or fear.

The judgment of law is the verdict of reason; the judgment of a single man is the result of reason and passion. The decision of a ruler, although just, is seldom above suspicion, envy, and opposition; the law does not labor under these handicaps. A government by law remains constant for a considerable time; the mind of an individual may change easily and frequently. Government by law may be reduced to an art; government by a monarch may lead to despotism. In general, the government of a regent himself is considered better than that of a vicar or agent; but government without laws requires many vicars who judge according to the mind of the ruler; a government by law, however, reflects the judgment of the supreme authority directly."[27]

The democratic principle of legal limitation and constitutional representative government, which was part and parcel of mediaeval monarchy, received much theoretical development in the doctrine of Cardinal Bellarmine.

He defended the practice which set legal boundaries to state power, and which restricted the monarch with all the powers of state that might be united in him, to constitutional limits. He struggled for the continuation of

---

[24] *De Laicis,* Cap. X.

[25] Proverbs 8:15.

[26] *De Laicis,* Cap. IX.

[27] *De Laicis,* Cap. X.

an institution, which the great Church councils had employed for eight centuries while educating Europe in the theory and practice of self-government; which a long line of deep and patient thinkers from Aquinas to his own time had upheld as the ideal of popular government; and which, traversing the ocean, became the cornerstone of American constitutional and representative government.

CHAPTER IV
ECCLESIASTICAL LIMITATION

The second general class of limitations upon temporal rulers during the Middle Ages was the spiritual power of the Church. The Middle Ages universally and freely acknowledged that the spiritual sovereignty of the Pope was of divine origin and direct institution, and that, in virtue thereof, the Pope, as the acknowledged guardian of the faithful, might, when the interests of religion and the rights of individuals and nations entered the domain of conscience, intervene even in matters of state. Any contrary opinion was regarded as a dangerous innovation.

Understood in the light of conditions prevailing in those times and in view of the relation then existing between Church and State, such a limitation was not at all unreasonable; nor did it, in any way, stunt the development and progress of national aspirations. It was a power which the Church used very sparingly.

The bare possibility, however, of any power, popular, constitutional, or ecclesiastical, presuming to place any curtailment upon the royal will, was distasteful to rulers of autocratic tendencies. Consequently, it was their constant effort to erase from the public mind of that day the tradition of this greatest check upon royal power.

William Barclay seems to have been one of the outstanding exponents of the new theory, for he drew from the pen of Cardinal Bellarmine a lengthy and complete refutation of all his arguments. The treatise of Barclay on the power of the Pope was not published until after his death.

So universal was the popular sentiment against this new and novel doctrine, that, in the opening sentence of his refutation of Barclay's book, Bellarmine writes: "Whoever it was who brought to light the book of William Barclay on the power of the Pope, dared not to give his name nor that of the printer nor the place of issuance, for he feared, and not without cause, that he would receive much censure and no praise.

"The author himself, if he now lived, would gladly conceal his name. And because Barclay universally denies every power of the Pope in temporalities, I shall show, without much labor, that such power has been and is universally recognized. Whether that power is absolute and direct, however, or whether it extends itself only in relation to spiritualities, we shall take under discussion."[1]

John Neville Figgis, in his treatise on Divine Right, states that "the dominant feeling at that time was that the supreme heresy of the Roman Church was the claim put forth on behalf of the papacy to a political supremacy over all kings and princes."[2]

Bellarmine, who lived in the midst of divine right theorists, set forth,

---

[1] *De Potestate Papae in Rebus Temp.* versus G. Barclaium, Praefatio.

[2] Figgis, *Divine Right of Kings,* p. 178.

in his treatise on the "Temporal Power of the Pope," that there were three opinions current on the power of the Pope in temporalities.

The first, he said, is that the Supreme Pontiff has, by divine right, "the fullest power over the whole terrestrial orb," both in ecclesiastical and in political matters. He admitted that "there were some few men like Augustinus Triumphus, Alvarus Pelagius, Panormitanus, Sylvester, and Hostiensis, who held this view. Hostiensis went so far as to maintain that by the advent of Christ all power of infidel princes was transferred to the Church, and resided in the Pope as the highest vicar of Christ, the true King, and that therefore the Pope could donate the kingdoms of infidels to any Christian ruler."[3]

Against this opinion Cardinal Bellarmine sharply set up the proposition that "the Pope is not the Lord of the whole world."[4] To show that he stood not alone in this contention, he quotes John of Turrecremata as saying, "The Pope cannot be said to have jurisdiction in temporalities by papal right, so that he could be called Lord of the whole world."[5]

Francis Victoria wrote, "The Pope is not the Lord of the whole world."[6] Bellarmine states that it is also generally recognized that "the Pope is not the Lord of such provinces as are under infidel rule, because the Lord committed to St. Peter only His own sheep, and infidels are not sheep of this fold. The Pope, therefore, cannot judge those outside his fold. 'What have I to do,' said St. Paul, 'to judge them that are without?'"[7]

In the twenty-second chapter of St. Matthew we read: 'Give to Caesar the things that are Caesar's.' Caesar must be another Lord. Since God has given the Pope no authority over infidel rulers, Lordship over the whole world would be an empty boast."[8]

Bellarmine goes a step farther and maintains that "the Pope is not even the spiritual Lord of the whole world. When all men will have been converted to the one true faith, then only, will the Pope become spiritual Lord of the whole world."[9]

Nor would Bellarmine admit that temporal princes were mere vicars or vassals of the Pope. "They do not derive their power from the Pope; the keys of the Kingdom of Heaven only, were given to St. Peter.

"A Christian king stands in no greater danger of losing his earthly realm, but rather does he possess a greater right to the eternal kingdom of heaven. Thus the Church publicly sings this hymn of Sedulius:

'Why fear, O Herod, wicked king, Christ's reign on earth below;

---

[3] Bellarmine, *De Romano Pontifice*, Lib. V, Cap. I.

[4] Ibid. Cap. II.

[5] Turrecremata, *Summa de Ecclesia*, Lib. II, Cap. 113.

[6] Victoria, *De Potestate Ecclesiae*, ques. 6.

[7] I Corinthians 5:12.

[8] Bellarmine, *De Romano Pontifice*, Lib. V, Cap. II.

[9] Ibid. Cap. III.

From thee no mortal thing takes He, who heaven's crown bestows.'[10]

"The temporal power has the king as its head,' said Hugo de St. Victor, 'the spiritual power has the Pontiff as its head,"[11] and John Driedo wrote: 'Christ, when He made Peter universal pastor of His Church, did not give to him temporal governorship over the universal Church, nor did He take from emperors and kings their kingdoms, nor did He wish that all regal power, like the ecclesiastical, be derived from the power of Peter."[12]

In further proof of the general acceptance of this view, he adduces the confessions of a number of pontiffs. "Pope Leo, in a letter to the Emperors Theodosius and Martin, states that the emperor is elected and that his authority is from God, not from the Pope."[13]

Popes Gelasius, Gregory I, Nicholas I, Alexander III, expressed themselves in similar terms. More at length, he quotes Pope Innocent III as declaring: "Why should we wish to usurp foreign power when we are not sufficient to exercise our own jurisdiction? We do not intend to judge concerning a fief, but concerning sin, which undoubtedly pertains to us. The Pope has full direct temporal power only in the patrimony of St. Peter, but not in other regions."[14]

Innocent compared the temporal and spiritual powers to the moon and the sun, upon which Bellarmine comments, "Note that the moon is not produced by the sun; both are the creations of God." If Pope Sixtus (1535-1581) feared to approve of Bellarmine's first volume *De Controversiis*, as some allege, on account of its frank declaration of an indirect power of the Pope in temporalities, Pope Gregory XIV granted Bellarmine's work a special approbation and promoted him to the highest honors in the Church.

From the common opinion of theologians, then, from the tradition of mediaeval history, the testimony of pontiffs, and from Holy Scripture, Bellarmine proves that the Pope is not the lord of the whole world, nor even the spiritual lord of the whole world, nor the temporal lord of the whole Christian world.[15]

There were others of the second opinion, like Calvin, Peter Martyr, and Brentius, who went to the other extreme and denied every right of the Church to exercise any influence or power in temporalities. They declared it unlawful that a pontiff or bishop should ever hold direct temporal governorship over any city or province, no matter by what just,

---

[10] Hostis Herodis impie, Christum venire quid times; non eripit mortalia, qui regna dat coelestia. Ibid. Cap. III.

[11] *De Sacramentis*, Lib. II, part 2, Cap. IV.

[12] *De Libertate Christiana*, Lib. II, Cap. II.

[13] *De Romano Pontifice*, Lib. V, Cap. III.

[14] Ibid., Cap. III.

[15] *De Romano Pontifice*, Lib. V, Cap. I, II, III.

free, or necessary title he might have acquired it. It was contrary to divine law, they said, that one man wield both the spiritual and the temporal sword.

Cardinal Bellarmine admitted and maintained that the Pope, as Pope, has no direct temporal jurisdiction over any city or province. In favor of this contention, he quotes John of Turrecremata, Cajetan, Navarrus, and others. Cajetan said, "The direct power of the Pope concerns spiritual things. The Pope has no direct temporal power. He has power in temporalities indirectly, that is, in so far as the spiritual good may demand interference in temporalities."

"There were some," Bellarmine relates, "who falsely held that Christ the God-Man was a temporal king, and from this erroneous principle two false doctrines were evolved: one, that the Pope, as Vicar of Christ, is both Pontiff and King; a second, that the king is both King and Pontiff, and that kingship is higher and more honorable than priesthood.

Kings, they claimed, are vicars of Christ the King; Pontiffs are Vicars of Christ the Highpriest; but Christ was more a King than a Pontiff because He descended from the royal tribe of Juda and the family of David, not from the tribe of Levi and the family of Aaron. As the Son of God," Bellarmine explained, "I grant that Christ always was a King and the Lord of all Creation, but this Kingdom is eternal and divine. Neither King nor Pope represents Christ in this capacity."[16]

He grants that "Christ is spiritual King of all men, believing and unbelieving; that Christ could, by virtue of His spiritual power, coordinate all temporal affairs to subserve the spiritual end; that Christ could have assumed royal authority, but that He did not assume it, for in no way did He preside over any temporal realm.

The Pope, therefore, as Pope and Head of Christ's Church has no temporal power. The king as king has no spiritual power. In the patrimony of St. Peter, the Pope has, of course, full temporal power in the same manner and by the same legitimate title as other rulers. Over other Christian countries and rulers, theologians attribute to the Pope only a spiritual power or an indirect temporal power."[17]

That the holding of direct temporal power by the Pope in particular instances, as in the Papal States, is not incompatible with the holding of spiritual power, and that under certain circumstances it may be beneficial to Church and State, the Cardinal deduces from examples in Holy Scripture.

"The first-born in the old law were kings and priests at once: Melchisedech, Moses, Noe, Abraham, Isaac, Jacob, Heli, were both temporal and spiritual rulers. Ecclesiastical and political powers are not contrary to each other. They both come from God; both are commendable; one serves the other; they overlap in many instances;

---

[16] *De Romano Pontifice*, Lib. V, Cap. IV.

[17] Ibid.

they are therefore not incompatibly vested in one person."[18]

"The third opinion, the more moderate, common, and Catholic opinion, holds that the Pope as Pope has no direct and immediate temporal power, but only a supreme spiritual power over all the faithful of his flock. By virtue of this spiritual power, he has an indirect power in temporalities. Followers of this more common opinion are: Hugo of St. Victor, Alexander Alensis, St. Bonaventure, Durandus, Peter of Alliaco, John of Paris, Jacobus Almair, Gabriel Biel, Henry de Gandavo, Joannes Driedo, John of Turrecremata, Albertus Piphius, Thomas Valdensis, Peter de Palude, Cajetan, Franciscus Victoria, Dominicus á Soto, Nicholaus Sanderus, Navarrus, Antonius Cordubensis."[19]

Concerning St. Thomas, Bellarmine is not so certain, but quotes him where he says, that "prelates can participate in wars, only in so far as wars affect the spiritual welfare."[20] In the face of this long list of authorities quoted by the Cardinal, one can scarcely hold the oft repeated assertion that the Popes of the Middle Ages arrogated to themselves complete, direct, and absolute temporal power over Western Europe.

By what right, then, did the Church exercise any political jurisdiction in the Middle Ages? This question Bellarmine answers in the sixth chapter of his treatise on the temporal power of the Pope. "The Pope," he says, "has only an indirect supreme temporal power; or, to speak more properly," he says elsewhere,[21] "the Pope has power in temporalities."

"This much is certain," he says, "and well recognized that the Supreme Pontiff can for a just reason, such as the salvation of souls, the freedom of religion, the conservation of the Church, judge in temporalities and even depose temporal princes."[22]

We must remember here that Bellarmine is speaking of Catholic princes whom the apostolic power of "binding and loosing" in matters of conscience may affect as fully as the lowliest subject. In virtue of this spiritual power, the Pontiff may bind the Catholic prince with the bond of excommunication; he may loose the subject of an excommunicated Christian king from the oath of fidelity and obedience; he may command the people to elect another king.

To understand the Church's political activities in those times, we must recall the relations then existing between Church and State. Since both provide for the welfare of one and the same subject—the Church, for the spiritual, the State, for the temporal—the relationship always upheld as ideal by the Church, and recognized by mediaeval kings and peoples, has been one of mutual cooperation, friendship, and union. An idea of

---

[18] *De Romano Pontifice*, Lib. V, Cap. IX.

[19] *De Romano Pontifice*, Lib. V, Cap. I.

[20] St. Thomas, 2, 2, ques. 40, art. 2.

[21] *De Potestate Papae in Rebus Temp.*, Cap. XIII.

[22] Ibid., Cap. III.

the relationship existing between Church and State at this time may be gathered from a description of it by Barclay and commented upon by Bellarmine."[23]

"Ecclesiastical and civil authority," Barclay maintained, "are, by divine right, distinct and separate." This Bellarmine admits to be true in the sense that Church and State have their own sphere of action, but he denies that the State is nobler and superior to the Church so that it might presume to direct, correct, or command the Church in spiritual matters. Church and State have separate and different functions, dignities, and offices, but they are not separated. Secondly, "Both come from God."

In Bellarmine's interpretation, the Church's power comes directly from God, the political power indirectly, by way of the consent of the people. Thirdly, "Each remains supreme and independent in its own sphere and must not transgress its bounds." Fourthly, "Neither has power over the other."

This last and fourth point Bellarmine would not admit without explanation. He quotes an ancient Canon which cites the words of Pope Gelasius to the Emperor Anastasius, to wit: "There are two powers by which the world is ruled: the sacred authority of the Pontiffs and the regal power of the sovereigns. The duties and dignities of the priesthood are the greater, because the priests are responsible to God, also for the right conduct of temporal government; but how can the Pontiff be accountable for the temporal government if, as Barclay maintained, he has no power whatsoever over them?"[24]

Bellarmine maintained that at times the temporal power must be subordinate to the spiritual, because the purposes of the temporal power are subordinate to the purposes of the spiritual. Figgis,[25] in comparing the Presbyterian theory as expounded by Cartwright with the papal contention as defended by Cardinal Bellarmine, seems to assume that Bellarmine regarded the state as the handmaid of the Church, the prince her executant, and his power as derived from the Church. None of these assumptions follow, however, from Bellarmine's doctrine of indirect temporal and supreme spiritual power of the Pope.

Note how Bellarmine distinguishes here between a two-fold subordination, direct and indirect. "A legate or delegate," he explains, "is a direct subordinate; he has derived power. An indirect subordinate does not derive his power from him to whom he is subordinate. The purpose merely of his work is subordinate. So the State is only an indirect subordinate of the Church; it does not derive its power from the Church, but from God, by the consent of the multitude. Whenever the course of the temporal authority does not subserve, at least remotely and indirectly, the spiritual welfare of men, but rather hinders it, then the

---

[23] Ibid., Cap. II.

[24] *De Potestate Papae in Rebus Temp.* Cap. II.

[25] *Divine Right of Kings*, pp. 188-190.

spiritual authority has a right, even a duty, to intervene."[26] The Cardinal thus illustrates his argument: "The art of government is different and distinct from the art of sculpture, oratory, astronomy, etc., nor are these derived from each other in any way; they are unique in their own spheres. The governor does not propose standards to the sculptor nor to the orator; still, these are subservient to good government.

'The ruler might command the sculptor not to produce obscene statues or pictures, which would corrupt the morals of his people. He might insist that the sculptor use no bronze or gold or silver, because these metals were necessary for the conduct of state. Nobody considers the limitation here placed by the ruler upon the sculptor, as meddlesome or unreasonable. Similarly, the higher and superior ends to be attained by the Church give her a right, not by virtue of any temporal power, but in view of her spiritual mission, to intervene."[27]

Again the Cardinal illustrates this principle by an analogy: "The body has feeling and appetite, which dictate such acts as are necessary to maintain the body in health. The soul has intellect and will, with corresponding functions to preserve the health of the soul. Body may exist without spirit, as is found in animals; spirit without body, as in angels. Neither exists primarily on account of the other.

In man, body and spirit are united, and because united, the one must be inferior, the other superior. While the spirit ordinarily does not mix in the operations of the body, it may, however, if the body work unto the detriment of the spirit, command it. It may impose fasts and penances, refrain the tongue from speaking, prevent the eye from seeing. Furthermore, if a positive act of the body becomes necessary to attain a definite end of the spirit, the spirit may demand that service.

Thus the political power has its princes, laws, decisions; the Church has its bishops, canons, and decrees;—the State, to maintain temporal order, the Church, to procure eternal salvation. They have existed, separated, as in the time of the Apostles, united, as at present. When united, they effect one body with inferior power subject to the superior. In this relation the spiritual power does not interfere in the temporal except for spiritual reasons, but if the spiritual needs the temporal it ought to have the right to demand its service.

The temporal power has a correlative right to the moral support of the spiritual. To take a concrete example: The Pope as Pope could not depose temporal princes, even for a just cause, in the same way as he could depose a Bishop, that is, as the ordinary judge in the case, but as supreme spiritual head, he could, if he found the rule of a certain prince harmful to the welfare of souls, declare him deposed and absolve his subjects from obedience. Again, the Pope as Pope could not ordinarily make civil laws because he is not a political prince, but if the civil rulers failed in such duty he might for the welfare of souls, by his

---

[26] *De Potestate Papae in Rebus Temp.* Cap. II.

[27] Ibid., Cap. II; and *De Rom. Pontif.* Lib. V, Cap. VI.

supreme spiritual power, frame or abrogate certain laws."[28]

"Whether or no the Popes from Gregory VII to Boniface VIII wielded an authority that was both despotic in its nature and oppressive in its incidence, it is certain that their despotism did not rest upon physical force, but upon purely spiritual and moral sanction. The Papacy never, as a matter of fact, wielded or claimed to wield the material sword."[29]

In case of conflict between ecclesiastical and civil legislation the rules to be observed are: "First, if the matter in question be one which jeopardizes the salvation of souls, the law of the emperor is abrogated by the law of the pontiff; second, when the matter in question is of a temporal nature, and not concerning the salvation of souls, then the pontiff's law does not abrogate the imperial law, but both are to be upheld, the civil law, in the civil courts, the ecclesiastical, in the ecclesiastical courts."[30]

"Absolutely speaking," Bellarmine concludes, spiritual power does more properly become the pontiff, and temporal power, the king."[31] But on account of the evil of those times, history proves amply that it was not only expedient but really necessary for the Pope to take a hand in the temporal affairs of those states during the period of their formation. "Such political jurisdiction of the Church," says Carlton J. H. Hayes, "had been quite needful and satisfactory in the period—from the fifth to the twelfth century, let us say—when the secular governments were weak and the Church found itself the chief unifying force in Christendom, the veritable heir to the universal dominion of the ancient Roman empire."[32]

The Popes and Bishops of the Middle Ages are sometimes pictured as autocrats, but Melanchton, one of the "Protestant reformers" of the sixteenth century, is quoted as admitting in a letter written after the din of that battle "should that I could not only confirm, but restore the power of the Bishops."[33] Renan, in the *Revue des deux Mondes* of March 1, 1880, admitted the beneficent influence of a central power like the papacy as an arbiter of the disputes of Europe.

Even Voltaire forgot his acrid humor against the Church long enough to write in his *Essai sur L'Histoire Générale* (ch. IX): "The interest of the human race requires a check to restrain sovereigns and to protect the lives of their people; this check of religion might in a general convention be placed in the hands of the Popes." "The fear of Papal excommunication undoubtedly tended to confine aggression within limits

---

[28] *De Romano Pontifice,* Lib. V, Cap. VI.

[29] Figgis, *Divine Right of Kings,* p. 198.

[30] *De Rom. Pontif.* Lib. V, Cap. VI.

[31] Ibid.

[32] Hayes, *Political and Social History of Modern Europe,* vol. 1, p. 125.

[33] Dunning, *Political Theories,* vol. 2, p. 22.

and to make rulers temper expediency with right reason."[34]

"The Church," says Lecky, "which often seemed so haughty and so overbearing in its dealings with kings and nobles, never failed to listen to the poor and to the oppressed, and for many centuries their protection was the foremost of all the objects of its policy."[35] "The mediaeval papacy saved Europe from anarchy and lawlessness."[36] "The influence of the Popes was a blessing to mankind."[37]

Guizot in his *History of Civilization in Europe* admits: "When a pope or bishop proclaimed that a sovereign held lost his rights, that his subjects were released from their oath of fidelity, this interference, though undoubtedly liable to the greatest abuses, was often, in the particular case to which it was directed, just and salutary...

"In the tenth century, the oppressed nations were not in a state to protect themselves, to defend their rights against civil violence—religion, in the name of Heaven, placed itself between them."[38]

The Protestant philosopher, Leibnitz, speaking of a project of arbitration proposed in his day, wrote:

"Somebody proposed the city of Lucerne as the seat of a court of arbitration; as for me, I am of the opinion that such a court should be set up in Rome itself to settle the quarrels of princes, and that the President of it should be the Pope, since in other times he exercised the office of Judge among Christian princes."

Practically all historians of note and the civilized world, of the past as well as of the present, realize that a wise and prudent limitation of political power is beneficial to the wellbeing of the State. It may serve both as an inspiration and a check to the sovereign.

Against the unwholesome movement of absolute and unrestricted power Cardinal Bellarmine upheld the traditional view of constitutional and ecclesiastical limitation, which, rightly understood, is as correct today as it was then.

All fair minded governments of the civilized world tacitly admit, rather than explicitly express, the importance and the necessity of the rights and prerogatives enjoyed by the Church in the State. It is a relationship and friendship taken for granted rather than formally defined.

The sentiment of humanity resents a government that is inimical to the wholesome influence of the Church. Pope Leo XIII, in his encyclical *Immortale Dei,* says:

"There was a time when states were governed by the principles of the Gospel. Then Church and State were happily united in concord and

---

[34] Figgis, *Divine Right of Kings*, p. 186.

[35] Lecky, *Rationalism in Europe*, vol. 2, p. 231.

[36] Fisher, *History of the Reformation*, ch. 2, p. 32.

[37] Wheaton, *History of the Laws of Nations*, p. 33.

[38] Guizot, *History of Civilization in Europe*, p. 149.

friendly exchange of good offices. Could not such a happy condition be repeated? Could not the Church and State be independent in their respective spheres and be of mutual help to each other ? Why should there be a conflict, since both come from God? Are we less wise than our forefathers were? Let there be cooperation between Church and State."

CHAPTER V
INTERNATIONAL RELATIONS

The new political theory and the politico-religious revolt against the papacy in the sixteenth century freed the sovereign from every accountability to the community or the Church. There remained no check upon his greed and ambition to expand and aggrandize his own realm at the expense of a weaker and smaller nation. Up to this time the Pope had served, in the last analysis, as the supreme and international court where the differences between kings and nations were adjusted. "As an arbitrator between states, the Pope often possessed great influence for good. In an age of force he introduced into the settlement of international disputes principles of humanity and justice."[1] "The papacy, whatever might be said against it, was at least a standing witness to the need of international morality, and might be supposed to have the advantage of viewing political problems from a universal standpoint."[2]

The nations had been bound together in the common union of Catholicism and were largely guided by the Canon Law of the Church, but now "the Canon Law," says Figgis, "ceased, in fact, to be international, which it most distinctly was in the Middle Ages."[3]

"By bridging the power of the Popes," says Balmes, "both people and government were let loose from that gentle curb which restrained without oppressing, and corrected without degrading; kings and people were arrayed against each other without any body of men possessed of authority to interpose between them in case of a conflict; governments began to place their reliance upon standing armies, and the people upon insurrections."[4]

While the twentieth century has readopted practically all the political ideas which the Reformation discarded, the only important factor in pre-Reformation political adjustment which the modern world has definitely refused to reintroduce is papal international arbitration. In its place we are attempting to set up a rather dubious League of Nations.

After the papal authority was removed, there was no longer any higher power to prevent infringement upon the territory, rights, and resources of other nations. Consequently, the formulation of international laws and checks became imperative at this time. Hugo Grotius, who was born in 1583 and died in 1645, is well known in history as the Father of international law. He devoted his whole life to the study and development of international relations.

It is among the theological moralists, however, that we find the first students of international law. The Spanish theologian, Vasquez, as early as

---

[1] Lawrence, *Principles of International Law*, p. 34.

[2] Figgis, *Divine Right of Kings*, p. 186.

[3] *Gerson to Grotius*, p. 123.

[4] *European Civilization*, p. 390.

1564 formulated principles of reciprocal rights between free states. Suarez speaks of the inter-dependence of nations according to the laws customarily recognized by the nations. Cardinal Bellarmine enjoys no reputation as an exponent of international law, like Grotius or Vattel. These two men lived a little later than Bellarmine when international questions became more acute.

To Cardinal Bellarmine is due, however, a considerable share of the credit which is justly conceded to the work of the Jesuits in laying the foundation of later international law. "The *De Jure Belli et Pacis* was possible," says Figgis, "because the Jesuits had helped in popularizing a way of looking at law which insisted on its ethical content and regarded it as the embodiment of reason."[5]

"Their treatises are full of the idea of the law that is more than national," and "by their frank recognition of the separateness, independence, and national freedom of states, combined with their belief in the law natural as the basis of all law, and with their inheritance of civil and canon law from the Middle Ages, the Jesuits of the sixteenth century prepared the way," and their theory "was to take the form of international law in the next century. Their system is at the very bottom of the system of Grotius."[6]

Grotius, in that next century, "based all his international law upon the bond common to all men, human reason, or natural law."[7] The lingering conception of Christian unity inherited from the Middle Ages, which was now to be reconciled with the independence of national units and the impossibility of making the Pope or the emperor international arbiters, called forth a demand for some other rule of interstatal relations, for which the Catholic theologians by their recognition of political facts combined with ancient ideals of unity laid the foundation. "Before international law fell into the hands of Grotius and his followers, it had like most other subjects of thought, attracted the attention of Roman Catholic theological writers."[8]

While the Cardinal did not write professedly on international relations, it will be interesting to note that what he did have to say on this subject was again in accord with the broad spirit evidenced in his principles of democracy. His treatise on *The Offices of Princes*, written in 1618, reveals the fact that this question was growing more acute even in his day, and he lays down such principles as have been fundamental in international law since the time of Grotius. "I have written this book on *The Offices of Christian Princes*," he remarks in the opening sentence, "not by my own volition, but by the request of those whom I could not refuse."

"Rulers have obligations to each other," he says. Discoursing on their mutual relations, he admonishes the more powerful princes "to conserve peace and to observe Christian charity towards weaker princes over whom they possess no rights, since the weaker prince or nation is also independent. There are rulers who, ignoring the true God and never having tasted the

---

[5] Figgis, *Trans. Royal Hist. Soc.*, xi, 107.

[6] Figgis, *Gerson to Grotius*, pp. 152, 164, 166.

[7] Introduction to Grotius' *Right of War and Peace*, David J. Hill, p. 9.

[8] Henry Sumner Maine, *International Law*, p. 13.

sweetness of divine charity, feign themselves to be glorious if they subject some weaker nation to their rule. Such kings truly conduct themselves, not as men, but as beasts of the forests. In the animal world strength prevails over weakness; the lion, by some right of his own, kills the wolf; the wolf devours the sheep; the sheep eats the herb. Thus Nimrod, when he became strong on earth and reigned in Babylon and subjected the neighboring nations, was called by Holy Scripture a 'strong hunter' because he captured men like prey. But, men, endowed with human reason, are born free and cannot be subjected one to the other except by just titles, such as election, succession, and others known to all."[9]

"Nebuchadnezzar took counsel with his Satraps to subject the whole world to his sway, and so informed Cilicia and Damascus and Libanus and Galilee and Jerusalem. He was much aggrieved to learn that they resented his domination. The Turks, followers of Mohammed, are so filled with the passion to rule that they would subject the whole of the Roman Empire to their sway were they not repelled by a similar passion in the Persians and Christian princes. Such barbaric conduct should be far from a Christian ruler who has before himself the most holy law of God, which prescribes Christian charity and faith unfeigned. A more powerful prince must not, for any reason, or under any pretext. oppress a weaker ruler, even though such proceeding be easily within his power.

"St. Augustine, in the fifth book, twenty-sixth chapter, of his *City of God* relates that when Valentinian the Younger, the colleague and co-regent of Theodosius in the Roman Empire, was exiled by Maximus the Tyrant, Theodosius might, without any resistance, have removed Valentinian from the co-regency, and held the universal empire for himself. He refrained from doing this, however, because he was a conscientious and Christian ruler. He rather restored to Valentinian his part of the empire and gave him good counsel. This is the law of charity and justice."[10]

"There are six ways," Cardinal Bellarmine observes in another work, "in which men are accustomed to acquire and possess kingdoms and empires: first, by the right of war: second, by divine benefice or singular call from God; third, by hereditary succession; fourth, by voluntary election; fifth, by gift of the head ruler; sixth, by decree of the highest head of the whole Church.

"War is not the only way of acquiring sovereign authority. The kingdom of the Jews, for example, was transferred from the house of Juda to the house of Levi, not by war, but by consent of the people. The transfer of the Merovingian empire to the Carolingians was made by the authority of the Pope and the consent of the 'Procerum,' and without arms. The Roman

---

[9] *De Officio Principis,* Cap. XXI. How closely this principle coincides with the declaration of President Wilson in his address to Congress, Feb. 11, 1918: "People may now be dominated and governed only by their own consent...people and provinces are not to be bartered about from sovereignty to sovereignty as if they were chattels and pawns in a game."

[10] *De Officio Principis,* Cap. XXI.

Imperium was transferred from the Greeks to the Franks under Charlemagne by authority of the Pope, and again from the Franks to the Saxons under Otto, with tranquility and without the sword. To wage war upon an unmolesting people, St. Augustine calls 'highway robbery."[11]

While Cardinal Bellarmine was a lover of peace and well disposed to conciliatory measures, yet he would not go so far as to condemn war as wrong and unnecessary in any and every instance. If one state or people suffered an injury from another, or was vexed by its maladministration, the injured state might seek redress or insist upon a change of policy. If all conciliatory measures failed, arms might even be resorted to and the incorrigible ruler deposed.

Both Bellarmine and Grotius maintained that all war is not in itself, and necessarily, repugnant to nature, nor to Holy Scripture. "It was an ancient heresy of the Manicheans," declared Bellarmine, "which condemned all wars as unlawful by their very nature, and which regarded Moses, Josue, David, and others as wicked men because they waged war. In our own time, "he continues, "Erasmus, Cornelius Agrippa, John Ferus, the Anabaptists, and others have revived the same heresy and contend that war was totally forbidden by Christ and the Apostles to Christians.

"We, however, teach what the whole Church has always taught by word and example, that war is not by its very nature unlawful for Christians, so long as the conditions to be noted later are observed."[12] As scriptural proof he cites the answer of St. John the Baptist to the soldiers who asked him, "What shall we do?" (to be saved). He answered, "Do violence to no man, neither calumniate any man, and be content with your pay."[13] "He did not command them," remarks Bellarmine, "to quit their station as soldiers. Again the Savior did not reprove the centurion who said, 'I have under me soldiers, and I say to this one "Go" and he goeth, and to another "Come" and he cometh,' but he commended his faith."[14]

"Cornelius, the centurion of the Italian band, is called in the Acts of the Apostles, a religious man, fearing God. One of his soldiers is also described as fearing the Lord. Tertullian, St. Basil, St. Gregory Nazianzen, St. John Chrysostom, St. Ambrose, St. Augustine, Pope Gregory I, St. Bernard, all taught that there had always been Christians, very saintly and pleasing to God, who served as soldiers, some even under pagan rulers, as for instance, the Theban legion of St. Maurice. Eusebius narrates how God assisted Constantine the Great by an evident miracle to gain the victory of war."[15]

Scripture texts like "Revenge is mine," and "I will repay," Bellarmine explains as referring to personal vengeance which is the Lord's. "The vengeance which public officials in authority carry out by law or legitimate warfare is the vengeance of the Lord. War is but the instrument of His

---

[11] *De Translatione Imperii Romani,* Cap. VII.

[12] *De Laicis,* Cap. XIV.

[13] Luke 3:14.

[14] Matthew 8:9.

[15] Bellarmine, *De Laicis,* Cap. XIV.

wrath."[16]

"God often uses the ill will (which He himself does not cause) of some men to punish the sins of others, and by an admirable disposition of His Providence, He sometimes takes kingdoms from some, and gives them to others. While he who succumbs to an invader may fall most justly, he who invades will possess that kingdom unjustly."[17]

The prophecy of Isaias, "Nation shall not lift up sword against nation, neither shall they be exercised any more to war,"[18] he explains with St. Jerome as referring to the time of the birth of Christ. "This prophecy was fulfilled in the reign of peace under Caesar Augustus. These words are merely a prophecy and not a prohibition."[19]

"The counsel given by the Lord, 'if any one strike thee on the right cheek, turn to him also the other,'[20] shows the spirit in which an individual private person should bear ignominy. Wars and the decrees of judges are not private, but public concerns."[21]

While the Cardinal does not prohibit war in every instance, observation of the conditions laid down by him and the scholastics would, in most instances, prevent war. He outlined under what conditions, by whom, in what manner, and when a nation might lawfully resort to war. Grotius followed Bellarmine and the Catholic theologians very accurately in demanding these same conditions.

The leading question in the first book of Grotius' work is: Whether any war be just and what constitutes the justice of that war. Many questions examined by him had received thorough discussion in the works of Bellarmine, twenty-five to forty years previously. Bellarmine's works were well known and widely read in the days of Grotius.

In the fifteenth chapter, *De Laicis,* and later in the twenty-first chapter of his *De Officio Principis,* the Cardinal enumerates the four conditions generally recognized to be necessary for lawful, just, and humane conduct of war:

"The first condition is legitimate authority to declare war. According to the common consent of men, such authority resides in all rulers and peoples who are not politically subject to higher authority." He quotes St. Augustine as saying in his work against Faustus, 'the natural judgment of mankind, which is ardently devoted to peace, demands that war be declared by such only as are clothed with sovereign authority.' "Private subjects can appeal to a higher court, but an independent and sovereign ruler has no such recourse.

"In aggressive warfare, supreme authority is required. For defensive warfare, the highest authority is not necessary because any one, even a

---

[16] *De Laicis,* Cap. XVI.

[17] Bellarmine, *De Trans. Rom. Imp.*, Lib. I, Cap. 7.

[18] Isaias 2:4.

[19] *De Laicis,* Cap. XIV.

[20] Matthew 5:39.

[21] *De Laicis,* Cap. XIV.

private citizen, has a right to defend himself when attacked." Grotius practically restates the same thought when he divides war into three classes: public, private, and mixed. "Private warfare is not so readily justified," he says, "since a private subject may have recourse to a higher tribunal, yet," he states that "there may be cases in which private redress must be allowed if the way to legal justice be barred. Public warfare must be made by the sovereign power of the state and must ordinarily be accompanied by certain formalities. In case of resistance, any magistrate seems to have the right to take up arms to maintain his authority and to defend his people." [22]

"A powerful ruler," says Bellarmine, "is not a good judge, however, concerning the justice of his own cause against a weaker ruler. His desire of expansion may influence him to presume a good cause to be present, when in reality it does not exist. Nor can he rely too much upon his own domestic counselors. Foreign, disinterested, and impartial judges are better qualified to make such decisions.

"Governments should manifest much good will in their diplomatic relations. While proper deference may demand certain formalities, great and magnanimous princes have very laudably and with much credit to themselves dispensed with such formalities."

The Cardinal relates an example in the relations of the Emperor Henry I with Robert, King of the Franks. "When the question arose whether the King ought first approach the Emperor, or the Emperor the King, their counselors had decided that the two should meet midway in the stream. The Emperor, however, of his own accord approached the King first, and was most magnanimously received. The next day the King came to the Emperor in order to continue the negotiations, and a satisfactory peace was arranged. Both were truly religious and Christian men. Let Christian nations imitate their example, and not insist upon many vain and really worthless ceremonies which might bring upon a people heavy burdens of sorrow, grief, and death. Certainly, Christ our Lord was not only our Master and Teacher but also our King and Emperor. To imitate Him cannot be dishonorable, but most proper. But He was not inflated with pride when extolled, nor depressed with discouragement when reviled." [23]

"As a second condition for legitimate warfare a just, grave, certain and not doubtful cause is required." A very serious injury must have been suffered from another ruler or people that is sovereign and independent. Cardinal Bellarmine, in stating this second condition, again quotes St. Augustine, who in his *Book of Questions on Josue* defines just wars as the "ultimate means of avenging the injuries suffered at the hand of an offending nation or city which neglects to vindicate what has been maliciously perpetrated by its government or its subjects, or which refuses to restore what has been wrongfully taken away." In support of this contention Bellarmine continues: "A sovereign is not the ordinary judge over foreign subjects, nor has he any way of punishing them; but he has a right in defense of his own subjects to pass judgment over offending aliens to the extent of punishing by war those

---

[22] Grotius, *De Jure Belli et Pacis*, Bk. 1, Ch. III.

[23] *De Officio Principis*, Cap. XXI.

who have inflicted grave injury on his subjects.[24] Unless the injury be very serious, however, and far reaching, the harm resulting from war," he says, "will be greater than the original injury, which was to be repaired or averted."

The great Spanish Dominican, Francis de Victoria, applies this test very rigorously when he says, "No war is just if it is admitted that it involves more harm than good for the state, even though on other counts there are titles and reasons for a just war. . . . Indeed, since one state is a part of the whole world .... if war is useful for one province or state, yet harmful to the world or to Christendom, then I believe that by that very fact the war is unjust."[25] Conceding this principle, it will be difficult to justify war in very many instances.

Again, "the justice of a cause must be certain and not doubtful. If the cause be doubtful, a distinction is to be made between the sovereign authority and the soldiery. The sovereign, if he proceeds to war, doubtful of the injury or of its maliciousness, sins gravely.

War is an act of vindictive justice, and it is grossly unjust to punish a whole nation for a crime not certainly proved." Bannez, the disciple of Victoria, binds the ruler who intends to declare war to a most careful previous examination of all the facts and grievances involved on both sides. If he cannot do this without consulting the other ruler, he is bound to send ambassadors to him to ask that the whole case be investigated by judicial arbitrators. In criminal charges against citizens, he says, the judge ought to proceed with the greatest care.

But war is an act of vindictive justice in a most serious criminal case. Therefore, there ought to be a most careful examination. Such preliminary proceedings may seem idealistic and unpractical, but, says O'Rahilly,[26] "Contrast, for instance, the elaborate, impartial proceedings which mark a great trial, or an investigation into some railway accident, with the secret machinations, underhand plotting and concocted frenzy which usher in a world devastating war, fraught with death and torture for millions of our fellowmen.

"The literal truth, is, of course, that nowadays there is immeasurably more judicial and impartial investigation in trying the case of a single criminal than in declaring war on a whole people. The judicial concept of war is practically defunct...The most solemn and serious judicial act that any nation can perform—a declaration of war against another community of human beings—is still shrouded in the mists of secret diplomacy, is initiated by a handful of partisans, is pursued for undiscoverable or unjustifiable objects, and is paid for by the sacrifice of all that is precious and noble in life."

The Cardinal also lays down some rules to be followed by soldiers in doubtful warfare. "Soldiers," he says, "do not sin by participating in a doubtful war unless it be evidently and certainly proved to be unjust.

---

[24] *De Laicis*, Cap. XV.

[25] *Rel. Theol.*, iii, 13.

[26] *Studies*, June 1918, p. 235.

Subjects must obey a superior and may not dispute his commands. Rather should they presume his cause to be good, unless they clearly know the contrary.

"When the guilt of an individual is doubtful, the judge who condemns him sins, but not the executioner who puts the condemned man to death, for the executioner is not bound to examine the sentence of the judge. This rule, however, pertains only to subject soldiers and to those who have long served the king and enjoyed his support in time of peace.

"Foreign soldiers, who are enlisted for a particular war and who owe no national allegiance to the contending sovereign or nation, cannot proceed to battle with a good conscience unless they know that this particular war in which they are to be engaged is just. Those who give this matter no thought, but are ready to fight for pay, whether the war be just or not, stand in danger of eternal condemnation."[27]

Bannez maintained the same, and Cardinal Cajetan said, "Such men are manifestly in the state of eternal damnation."[28] According to these principles, then, a soldier, if he can assume that his government is actuated by Christian principles, may with good conscience leave the matter of a careful examination into the justice of a war to his superiors. While this principle would be hard to apply in an anti-Christian environment of war, "it is vital to assert," says Alfred O'Rahilly, "this right of conscience for that small minority who take seriously the question of the liceity of war."[29]

Suarez says, "If the reasons showing the war to be unjust are such that they cannot answer them, they are bound in some way to investigate the truth, though this burden must not be lightly imposed, unless these reasons render the justice of the war very doubtful."[30]

"The third condition for a justifiable war is the right intention. Since the purpose of war," says Cardinal Bellarmine, in discussing this third condition, "is public peace and tranquility, it is not lawful to wage war for any other purpose. Hence, not only Kings but soldiers sin gravely, if they undertake war to injure others, to extend their empire, or to exercise warlike courage, or for any other cause except the common good—even though neither legitimate authority nor a just cause be lacking."[31]

"In his book against Faustus, St. Augustine wrote, 'The desire to injure, the cruelty of revenge, the implacable ferocity of bestial warfare, the craving to dominate and the like, these are the things culpable in warfare and rightly censured.' In his epistle to Boniface, St. Augustine said, 'The will must have peace in mind; necessity alone can force war. Nor may the desire of peace be pretended in order that war might be waged, but war is waged that peace may be attained. Be pacific, therefore, even in warring, so that you may lead

---

[27] *De Laicis,* Cap. XV.

[28] *Summula,* s. v. "bellum," (Duaci, 1627, p. 30).

[29] *Studies,* June, 1918, p. 238.

[30] *De bello,* vi, 9.

[31] *De Laicis,* Cap. XV.

those whom you oppose to the unity of peace."[32]

"Two points are here to be noted," the Cardinal continues. "Since war may be undertaken only as a means of obtaining peace, and since this means is most dangerous and expensive, it remains that war must be employed but sparingly and reluctantly. In proof of good will and a right intention, every other conciliatory means, such as peacefully requesting condign satisfaction from the enemy, must first be attempted. 'When you go out to attack a city,' wrote Moses in Deuteronomy, 'first offer it peace. Perchance the enemy state would prefer to make fullest satisfaction rather than hazard the fortunes of war."

"The question is sometimes raised," he observes: "What if the enemy at first refuses satisfaction, but shortly after the war has begun sues for peace and offers reparation? Is the opposing side bound to desist from further prosecution of the war?" He quotes Cardinal Cajetan as maintaining that there is no obligation to desist after the inception of the war, but there was an obligation to accept reparation before the war. "But it seems," Bellarmine replies himself, "that, in the absence of a better solution, there is no obligation in justice of accepting reparation before or after the clash of arms, if a truly just cause evidently existed.

"In charity, however, there is almost always such an obligation before and after the war has begun. A sovereign having just cause for war assumes the capacity of judge over the offending sovereign. But a judge is not bound to condone the death sentence of a culprit, even though satisfaction be offered. In mercy, he could make the condonation if he was the supreme judge.

"A king, for example, could, in mercy, but he is not obliged, in justice, to spare the life of a thief, although the ill-gotten goods were restored. The reason for arguing an obligation in charity is the fact that war is a most terrible ordeal which punishes not only those who have offended but many innocent parties.

"Christian charity would therefore dictate cessation of war when proper satisfaction is offered. In an extreme case, however, the enemy might be of such a nature that his subjugation or complete destruction would be expedient for the common good. Such enemies were, for instance, the Amorrhites, whom God commanded to be completely destroyed."[33]

"In the second place," Bellarmine says "it is to be noted that this third condition differs from the two preceding ones in this, that if the first two conditions be lacking, war is unjust. If this third condition be wanting, war would be malicious, but not unjust. He who without authority and without a just cause promotes war sins not only against charity but also against justice, and he is no longer a soldier, but a thief.

He who has authority and a just cause but battles rather for the love of revenge and of extending his empire, or for any other wicked reason, acts

---

[32] Ibid.

[33] Deuteronomy 20:13.

contrary, not to justice, but to charity. He is not a thief, but a bad soldier."[34]

"As a corollary it follows that when this third condition is wanting, neither the soldier nor the king are obligated to restitution, but only to repentance. But if the first and second condition be wanting, all are bound to restitution for the damage done, unless excused by invincible ignorance. Gross and culpable ignorance would not excuse from restitution. If one discovered later that the war was, after all, unjust, he is not obliged to repair the damage done during the war, but to restore anything he might have carried away. If he possesses nothing in particular of the former enemy's property, but has grown richer over the war, he is obliged to make reparation to the extent of his increased riches. Another's goods cannot be retained, even though they were acquired in good faith and without sin, but they must be given either to the owner or, if he be unknown, to the poor."[35]

Wars are often begun with the most humanitarian motives and for the noblest of causes, but too often they degenerate into the abyss of most un-Christian hatred, revenge, greed, cruelty, and conquest, which vitiate the former good intention and place the war in the category of the unlawful.

The fourth condition laid down by Cardinal Bellarmine and the scholastics demands that the manner of warfare be "legitimate, reasonable, and humane." Grotius, in his third book of the *Rights of War and Peace,* asks what is lawful in war. "Under this head the general and principle rule to be observed," says Bellarmine "is that no innocent person receive any injury. War should be prosecuted in such a manner as to punish only those who deserve to be justly punished."

From the words of St. John the Baptist, as recorded in the third chapter of the Gospel according to St. Luke, Bellarmine derives a mode of conduct for soldiers. 'Do violence to no man,' said John, 'neither calumniate any man; be content with your pay.' The admonition, 'Do violence to no man,' prohibits injuries perpetrated in open violence, like the killing of peasants if they refuse to obey. It often happens that soldiers force others to perform difficult tasks, to prepare meals, to vacate their homes, or to serve them like slaves.

"These and many other things are comprehended in these words, 'Do violence to no man,' that is, force no man to do or to suffer that which by no right he is obliged to endure. 'Neither calumniate any man.' Soldiers often accuse a passerby of being a thief, a spy, an enemy, or a trespasser, and without reason or justice they despoil him, wound or kill him, or take him captive. Since these unfortunates can offer no proof of their innocence, they are compelled to redeem themselves by a large ransom and to suffer great vexation.

"A good ruler must endeavor to prevent such malpractices in war. 'Be content with your pay' prohibits any injury inflicted upon the goods of a person, as to steal or rob from anybody, or to make extortionate demands. Soldiers should be given sufficient remuneration so that they would have no cause to prey upon the citizenry for their needs. Rulers have an obligation to compensate their soldiers properly and then soldiers should be satisfied and

---

[34] *De Laicis,* Cap. XV.

[35] Ibid.

not molest strangers."[36]

"There are three classes of people," he says, "who should enjoy immunity from the ravages of war. First, all are to be excepted who do not belong to the enemy. Hence, soldiers cannot be excused who vex, despoil, injure, strike, take captive those through whose territory they pass. Often they return evil for good to those with whom they lodge. Nor can they be excused on the plea of insufficient support, for the goods of those who have not injured them can in no way be appropriated by the soldiers. The rights of neutral nations must be respected. Soldiers should pay for what they take. The natives are not obliged to pay taxes or penal fines to soldiers because their own government does not properly support them."

"To the second class belong such as are indeed of the enemy's number but are exempted by venerable custom and law of all nations. Among these are priests, monks, clerics, strangers, merchants, peasants passing to and fro or working in the fields, and their animals with which they till the soil."

"The third class universally exempted are they who are unfit for war. Minors, women, old men, and others unable to carry arms are not to be molested. While these, if they belong to the enemy, may be taken captive and despoiled of their goods, they certainly cannot be killed, unless this happens by accident, as if, for instance, a soldier shot upon troops and accidentally killed a boy, a woman, or a cleric.

"God himself commanded the Hebrews that when they waged war they spare the young and women. Humanitarian reasons dictate that there can be no reason to kill those who cannot fight. Nor can one argue that God himself is recorded in Holy Scripture as having commanded the slaying of infants and women and animals. What God, the Author of life commands, is to be done without questioning; no man can ask Him, 'Why do you act thus?' In the case of the Amorrhites we saw the reason for such general destruction."

Grotius, in discussing what is lawful in war, similarly writes, "Women and children should be spared, the aged, men whose modes of life are entirely remote from the use of arms, ministers of religion, who among all nations, from times of the most remote antiquity, have been exempted from bearing arms, husbandmen, who are common benefactors tilling the soil, merchants, artisans, and all others who cultivate the arts of peace should enjoy exemption from the vexations of war."[37]

These are the conditions of just warfare as propounded by the schoolmen of the later Middle Ages and restated by Cardinal Bellarmine. While Catholic philosophers do not declare all war in itself wrongful, the observance of these four conditions and all they imply would practically exclude most of the world's wars and would mitigate the cruelties and injustices of the necessary, just, or unavoidable wars.

Alfred O'Rahilly remarks in his article on *The Catholic View of War*, "Is it not an inspiring help to all lovers of humanity to find that the Church, even at the zenith of her political power, upheld such a high and noble ideal of a

---

[36] *De Officio Principis*, Cap. XXI, *De Laicis*, Cap. XV.

[37] *Right of War and Peace*, p. 362.

just war ?"[38]

The above principles give us a fair estimate of the mind of Cardinal Bellarmine on the duties and rights of rulers towards one another, in peace and in war. His kindly plea for a mitigation of the world's woes and injustices, chief of which are the sorrows of war, is another evidence of his democratic interest in the welfare of all peoples.

---

[38] *Studies*, June 1918, p. 241.

CHAPTER VI
POLITICAL RIGHTS

Other democratic principles which Cardinal Bellarmine deduced from the doctrine of popular sovereignty were: the political right of a people to determine, in the first instance, and to change at a later date, the form and structure of its government; the right even to depose a despot, if the application of all peaceful measures failed. According to the Cardinal, these popular rights were always virtually retained by the multitude in conferring power upon a sovereign.

The general political theory of the Middle Ages insisted upon such rights. The Ghibelline writer agreed with the Guelph in holding that the nation appoints the monarch and that it must see to it that he obeys the constitution. Thinkers like St. Thomas Aquinas and Marsilius of Padua, though of hostile schools, agreed upon such fundamental political theory as the superiority of the law to the ruler, and the abridgement of royal power by the nation. To show that such political rights were deeply rooted in the mediaeval mind, Lord Acton quotes the Scottish Parliament, in the struggle between the House of Bruce and the House of Plantagenet, as proclaiming: "Divine Providence, the laws and customs of the country, and the choice of the people, have made him our king. If he should ever betray his principles, we shall treat him as our enemy, as the subverter of our rights and shall elect another in his place..."[1]

In the Middle Ages when Europe was Catholic, this right was sometimes exercised through the Church. The deposition of Childeric by Pope Zacharias was the earliest exercise of the deposing power. It was often referred to in the sixteenth century as conclusive proof that this power had been recognized in the past. Cardinal Bellarmine comments upon it at length in his treatise, *De Potestate Papae in Rebus Temporalibus*, against William Barclay.[2]

Pope Leo III transferred the Roman Empire from the Greeks to the Franks, and he crowned Charlemagne Emperor, not by any superior temporal power but by the acclamation of the people. Some few mediaeval writers insisted that the Pope exercised such right by a supreme and direct temporal power, but the more general opinion was, as noted above in chapter four, that the Pope intervened either by an indirect temporal power in the interests of religion or human happiness, or that he intervened as the recognized and delegated defender of the people and so merely declared an autocratic Christian ruler as deposed.

In the sixteenth century, divine right theorists labored against Pope and people to destroy this political right of the Middle Ages. They maintained that a ruler derived his title of sovereignty, not from the people, but from God, by a fundamental hereditary and indefeasible right, which no religion, no law, no defect could alter or diminish. "The right acquired by birth cannot

---

[1] *History of Freedom*, p. 36.

[2] Chapter IV.

be forfeited through any act of usurpation, by any incapacity in the heir, or by any act of deposition."[3] The people, having had nothing to do with constituting the king, can never have a right to resist him, or to change the government. They must be satisfied with God's allotment.

Against this theory, and in defense of the mediaeval doctrine, Cardinal Bellarmine, in the sixth chapter of his treatise, *De Laicis*, declared: "Particular forms of government exist by the law of nations; they are not determined by the Divine Law because it depends on the consent of the multitude to place over itself a king, consul, or other magistrate, and for a legitimate reason, they can change royalty into aristocracy or democracy or vice versa, as it was done in Rome." [4] "At first the Roman city-state had kings, then the people did away with kings and yearly created magistrates. As the rule of kings, so that of consuls, was considered just because it so pleased the people.... In the beginning a reign may even be tyrannical, violent and unjust, but if the usurper rules well, the people may approve of his rule by their consent."[5]

In other words, every people and nation, has a right to choose for itself the particular form of government most suitable to its needs and desires. As time and generations change these needs and desires may change; the former spirit and efficiency of the government may have deteriorated; consequently, "a people never transfers its power to a king so completely, but it reserves to itself the right of withdrawing it."[6] In his debate with Barclay on this subject, Bellarmine states with the same precision: "God grants kingdoms to men by way of the consent and the counsel of men. He can and He does change and transfer kingdoms from one race to another by means of the consent of the same people."[7]

Thus far Bellarmine defends the claim that every people has a right to determine the form and personnel of its own government in the manner which best promises to promote the social and individual development and welfare. De Castro, Covarruvias, Cajetan and Suarez supported the same traditional view that a government which is not based on the consent of the people is tyrannical. Whether credit can be given to the influences of the Schoolmen and Cardinal Bellarmine or not, it was upon a principle like theirs that the Declaration of our national independence was based. The Fathers of the Country enumerated the "legitimate reasons" which justified them in casting off a condition of colonial subjection and setting up an independent government and state. It was this same principle which President Wilson invoked in his "Fourteen Points," where he refers to the rights of smaller nations to choose their own form of government.

---

[3] Figgis, *Divine Rights of Kings*, p. 6.

[4] *De Laicis,* Cap. VI.

[5] *Recognito De Laicis,* Cap. VI.

[6] Populus nunquam ita transferat potestatem suam in regem quin illam sibi in habitu retineat. Bellarmine, *Apologia,* Cap. XIII.

[7] *Recognitio De Laicis*, Cap. VI, contra Barclaium, Cap. V.

The next question that naturally arises is: can a people go so far as to depose a ruler? Can it change a form of government by force? Is there ever such a right as that of revolt against a government once sanctioned by consent of the people? Briefly, Bellarmine's answer is: ordinarily, no; for legitimate reasons and in "certain cases," yes.

The discovery of the gunpowder plot in 1605, to which some incensed and imprudent Catholics like Robert Catesby and his followers were driven by violent persecutions, raised a volley of protest and vilification against the patriotism and loyalty of Catholics in England. The Jesuits, especially a Father Henry Garnet, were falsely accused of conniving at the plot.

In defense of the Church, of Father Garnet, and of the Catholics of the land, Bellarmine gives the accepted Catholic view on sedition and rebellion. He first quotes the Catholic doctrine as enunciated by the Council of Constance (1414) which condemned the following proposition: "Any tyrant can and ought to be killed lawfully and meritoriously by any one of his vassals or subjects, even by secret plotting, subtle scheming, or adulation, in spite of a given oath or contract, irrespective of a sentence or mandate from any judge." This proposition the Council condemned as heretical and punishable.[8]

The Cardinal then goes on to state that the power of a people to choose its ruler and to determine its government must be understood at the beginning of a reign. "After a temporary or permanent magistrate has been created," he says, "the people have no longer any authority over the magistrate; but the magistrate rather has royal power over the people; nor is it permissible without grave crime to oppose a legitimate ruler or to agitate sedition and rebellion. Who," he asks, "in the time of Luther was the author of so many peasants' taking up arms against the princes? Were they not the ministers of the reformed or rather the deformed religion of Luther? Not even our enemies dare say that Catholics were the authors of that sedition. Who attempted to take up arms and kill King Francis of France, his spouse, his mother, and brothers ? Were they not the evangelical brothers, encouraged by Calvin ? Who excited so many mobs in Scotland against the king and tried to introduce anarchy? Were they not the very ones who introduced the reformed religion of Calvin? The king himself openly attests this fact. Let him cease then to ascribe to Catholics what his own doctrinaires have taught."[9] Under ordinary conditions, therefore, rebellion and sedition are not lawful, once the people have given their consent and have conferred the political power on the ruler.

That "in certain cases" and for "legitimate reasons" the government can be changed, Bellarmine bases on the fact that a particular ruler or form of government is of human determination. Among the older theologians he quotes St. Thomas as holding the same opinion; among the more recent of his time, Dominicus De Soto, and the Canonist Navarrus.[10]

---

[8] *Apologia,* Cap. XIII.

[9] *Apologia,* Cap. XIII.

[10] *Recognitio De Laicis.*

Against Barclay he argued: "To obey and serve the king, in general, is by divine right, but to obey this or that particular king is by human arrangement. We are obliged by divine right to obey this king while he reigns, but there is no provision by divine right which prohibits his deposition. By divine right we obey a king while he is on the throne, but it is not of divine right that he remain on the throne as long as he lives. He might resign or be dethroned; in either case, he ceases to command obedience upon his removal."[11]

Bellarmine again recalls the example of the Roman Republic, "which first had kings; then, yearly magistrates; later, a consular government; and this kind of government, too, was praised by Sacred Scripture.[12]

"Again the same state returned to a monarchical regime which was not less just, since the Scriptures[13] command obedience to such a sovereign also."[14] He then professes to agree with the opinion of Navarrus who says that a people never so completely transfers its power to a ruler but that it virtually retains or reserves to itself the right actually to reclaim or "receive back" this power in "certain cases" and "for legitimate reasons."[15]

He also cites St. Thomas as holding: "If any society of people have the right of choosing a king for itself, it is not unjust if he be deposed by the same, or if his power be curbed, when by a royal tyranny he abuses his power."[16] Bellarmine's doctrine differs from that of Hobbes, who taught that the power once yielded to the sovereign can never be revoked.[17]

Grotius agreed with the theory of Bellarmine that a nation may choose its form of government, but he departed from Bellarmine's contention when he asked: "Why may not a whole people completely transfer its sovereign rights to one or more persons without reserving any portion to themselves?"[18] Suarez, in commenting on Bellarmine's reply to King James, draws attention to the fact that Bellarmine did not simply say that the people retained power "in habitu" for the exercise of any arbitrary acts and as often as they wish; but "with great limitation and circumspection he said, 'for legitimate reasons."[19]

---

[11] *De Potestate Papas in Rebus Temp.*, Cap. XXII.

[12] They (the Romans) had made themselves a senate house and consulted daily three hundred and twenty men, that sat in Council always for the people, that they might do the things that were right. I Mach.8: 15.

[13] Romans 13:2.

[14] *Recognitio De Laicis.*

[15] Navarrus non dubitat affirmare, numquam populum ita potestatem suam in regem transferre, quin illam sibi in habitu retineat ut in certis casibus etiam actu recipere possit." *Apologia*, Cap. XIII, or *Recognitio De Laicis.*

[16] *De Reg.* Lib I, Cap. VI.

[17] Cf. *Leviathan, De Homine,* Cap. IV.

[18] *The Rights of War and Peace,* Bk. I, Ch. III, Art. 8.

[19] *Defensio* iii, 3. 3.

Nowhere, however, does Bellarmine seem to enumerate these "legitimate reasons" for a change of government. St. Thomas,[20] whom Cardinal Bellarmine follows very closely, and a number of recent writers and moralists like Alfred O'Rahilly, Dr. Cronin,[21] and Dr. John A. Ryan,[22] generally lay down the following conditions under which even physical force may be lawful.

First, the oppression must be habitual, tyrannical and intolerable. Alfred O'Rahilly would make the people themselves the ultimate arbiter as to the actual existence of unbearable tyranny. In the absence of any super-national judiciary the "vox populi" becomes the highest available court. Second, other remedial means must have failed, legal and pacific means must have been ineffective. Third, there ought to be a reasonable probability of success, lest the oppression be increased. "If indeed a tyranny is not excessive, it is better to bear it for a time," says St. Thomas, "than, by acting against the tyrant, to be involved in many perils, which are worse than tyranny. For it may happen that they who rise against a tyrant do not prevail against him; and so the tyrant, being incensed, rages the more violently."[23]

Fourth, the revolt ought to be approved by the majority and by the best men of the land. According to De Vareilles-Sommieres: "It is not necessary that the majority of citizens should act; even a minority, if it is sufficiently strong, has the right of defending and saving the country."

Some political writers of our own time, such as Haller, Cronin, even Jesuit moralists like Taparelli, Liberatore, Meyer, Cathrein, seem to fear that the theory of Bellarmine and Suarez is dangerous to civil order and encourages revolution and sedition, like the doctrine of Rousseau.

There is a great difference, however, between the doctrines of Bellarmine and the social contract theory of a Rousseau. According to the former, political power is a natural and divine institution, intrinsically necessary for the wellbeing of society; according to the latter it is a mere human convenience existing by the compact and agreement of men. According to Bellarmine, particular political power is derived immediately from the people as a political community, but ultimately from God. According to Rousseau, political power rests solely on the contract between ruler and subject. It is ultimately derived not from God but from the sum of the individual sovereignties bestowed upon the ruler. Thus every one might fancy himself a founder of the state and interpret the terms of contract as he chose.

According to Bellarmine, obedience to lawful authority is binding in conscience; according to Rousseau "each one is united to all, but nevertheless obeys only himself and remains as free as before." This theory exerted a baneful influence at the time of the French Revolution for it could only destroy all lawful authority and throw society into a maelstrom of

---

[20] *Summa* 2, 2, q. 42 a2-3.

[21] *Science of Ethics*, II, 542.

[22] *Right of Self-Government*, p. 19.

[23] *De Reg.* Bk. I, Ch. VI.

confusion.

The remote cause of the French Revolution was not the theory of popular sovereignty as expounded by Bellarmine and his associates but rather the theory of divine right of kings. In England it cost Charles I his head.

In France the reign of Louis XIV in the second half of the seventeenth century brought this theory to its fullest fruition. He himself did most towards the destruction of the ancient regime. Under Louis XV, a king of inferior ability but as extravagant in royal pomp as his father, the French nation descended swiftly into the abyss of the Revolution of 1789. Bad kings, if only they are bad enough, are the greatest source of revolution.

Bellarmine, however, avoided the extremes, both of the divine right theorists as advocated by James and his theologian, Robert Filmer on the one side, and of the social compact theory of Hobbes and Rousseau on the other. Taparelli, who would allow only passive resistance, and this not to reject but to reform a tyrant, intimated that had men like Bellarmine and Suarez lived two centuries later and had they witnessed the havoc of the French Revolution, they would possibly have changed their views.

One might answer: Had Bellarmine and Suarez lived two centuries later to witness the rather literal embodiment of their principles into the Virginia Declaration of Rights, and into that memorable document, The American Declaration of Independence—could they live today to behold the magnificent structure raised upon the foundation of political theories such as they advocated--they would rather be inclined to reaffirm than to retract their view.

That revolutionary minds might wrest this doctrine to the disturbance of national order, is true; still, its general acceptance may not be nearly so dangerous as its suppression. Nor did Gregory XVI in his Encyclical *Mirari Vos* (1832) condemn this doctrine.[24]

He merely wished to condemn as revolutionary such theories, which under the guise of inalienable sovereignty attribute to the people the right of arbitrarily and unreasonably overthrowing established governments. Catholic authorities have never taught that resignation and prayer are the only means and remedies against oppression.

The above discussion leads to the conclusion that in the beginning a political community has, therefore, an absolute right to choose its ruler and to determine its form of government.

For legitimate reasons, the sovereign state retains and reserves within itself the right to change its ruler and form of government. Against a tyrannical and harmful regime a people may use force after all available means have been unsuccessfully employed.

---

[24] In *Mirari Vos,* he says, "divine and human laws cry out against those who by base plots of war and sedition try to undermine loyalty to rulers and to drive them from government."

The Political Philosophy of St. Robert Bellarmine

CHAPTER VII
CIVIL LIBERTY - HUMAN EQUALITY

Civil liberty has been variously conceived by political writers. Sometimes it is synonymous with political liberty or expresses but a shade of difference in meaning. In the previous chapter we have conceived of political rights as the rights of a whole people in relation to its sovereign or government, and as the rights of a colonial or subject nation against a superior state or nation. In this chapter we are treating of civil liberty as the right and duty proper to the individual citizen in immediate relation to the state of which he is a part, and to its government. We are thinking of liberty as personal freedom from undue restraint, force, or servitude. It is not exemption from rightful legal control.

"It consists in this," says Cardinal Bellarmine, "that one is free to choose the good and reject the evil. The law is manifestly not repugnant to true liberty; for its purpose is not to impede the choosing of good and the rejection of evil but to promote the exercise and enjoyment of liberty. The law can rightly be said to be the opponent of servitude and the protector of liberty."[1]

Human equality in its strictest sense is natural equality. It proclaims all men as of equal value before the Creator. "All men are equal," says Bellarmine, "not in wisdom or grace, but in the essence and species of mankind."[2]

Human equality holds all life as sacred; it gives equal prospect of happiness in this and the next world. In the Christian religion human equality is dignified as Christian equality. It is exemplified in the poverty of the manger of Bethlehem, and proclaimed by the world apostle St. Paul in his preachment, "there is neither Jew nor Greek, there is neither bond nor free, there is neither male nor female; for you are all one in Christ Jesus[3] ...There is no respect of persons with God."[4]

Human and Christian equality has been the constant ideal and practice of the Christian Church throughout the ages. "The history of the Middle Ages is the history of the gradual emancipation of man from every species of servitude, in proportion as the influence of religion became more penetrating and more universal. The Church could never abandon the principle of liberty by which she conquered pagan Rome."[5]

The revival of Caesarism, however, and the later theory of divine right, naturally tended to obliterate the rights and liberties, civil and religious, of the private citizen. The individual existed for the state. His liberty was subservient to the will of the sovereign. His being was submerged in the

---

[1] *De Laicis,* Cap. X.

[2] *De Laicis,* Cap. VII.

[3] Galatians 3:28.

[4] Romans 2:11.

[5] The footnote for this quote is missing from Fr. Rager's original, 1926 text.

great body of the state; his individual happiness and welfare were overshadowed by the grandeur and pomp of the realm. His dignity and value as a human being bore no comparison of equality with royal blood.

The supporters of the divine right theory elaborated on the power of the king and minimized the right of the private citizen. Subjects were bound to "passive obedience" and absolute "non-resistance," which implied that if the king's command was contrary even to the law of God, the subject might for conscience' sake refuse to obey; he might obey God rather than man, but he was expected to suffer passively the civil punishments imposed on him for such civil disobedience.

The following passage sets forth the doctrine in the language of the time: "When the king enjoins anything contrary to what God hath commanded, we are to obey God rather than man; but we must patiently suffer what the king inflicts on us for such refusal, and not, to secure ourselves, rise up against him."[6]

"It is obedience that writers of the sixteenth century insist on, nor did they leave a loophole for Papal interference by admitting the possibility of resistance in extreme cases. They dwelt upon the absolute duties of non-resistance in all cases."[7]

The Divine Right theorists insisted upon obedience absolute and immutable, or the Pope would find it possible to make good some part of his claim. Luther, Melanchthon, Zwingli, Calvin, all taught the severest type of passive obedience and absolute non-resistance.

"In the welter of Tudor absolutism, there was room for no more than a single doctrine of political theory and that was the doctrine of passive obedience." [8]

"By the dignitaries of the Anglican establishment, passive obedience was declared to be the whole duty of subjects."[9] Obedience was proven to be due the king as a divinely appointed governor. In Tyndall's 1528 work, *The Obedience of a Christian Man,* passive obedience is inculcated without any qualifications. Robert Barnes in his *Supplication to the Most Gracious Prince, Henry VIII* (1534), declares most emphatically in favor of passive obedience. In the reign of Elizabeth there are the strong assertions of Jewel in his *Apology for the Church of England* that, "obedience is due to princes and magistrates though they be very wicked."

In Heywood's *Royal King and Loyal Subject* (1600), the subject is portrayed as rendering unconditional obedience to the most unreasonable caprice of an arbitrary and unlimited royal authority.

Had the Church in the sixteenth century not protested against such absolute oppression and serfdom, she would have ceased to merit the title of

---

[6] *Whole Duty of Man,* Sunday xiv, 5. This passage is quoted by Hobbes as the 'doctrine of the king's party. ' (Behemoth, Part 1, p. 80).

[7] Figgis, *Divine Right of Kings,* p. 95.

[8] Wm. A. Dunning, *History of Political Theories From Luther to Montesquieu,* p. 206.

[9] Cf. Prothero, *Statutes and Constitutional Documents,* p. 435.

"protector of the people." Balmes asks very strikingly: "If supreme power makes a scandalous abuse of its faculties, if it extends them beyond their due limits, if it tramples on fundamental laws, persecutes religion, corrupts morality, outrages public decorum, attacks the honor of citizens, exacts illegal and disproportionate contributions; in such cases, does Catholicism prescribe obedience? Does it forbid resistance? In such extremities great theologians consider that resistance is lawful; the dogmas of the Church, however, do not descend to these cases."[10]

Against such abuse of political power Bellarmine maintains that absolute obedience is not an obligation in case of a bad and unjust law.[11]

He would also consider resistance lawful if the king attempts to draw his subjects into a false religion or infidelity; if his rule be harmful to the higher and supernatural welfare of his subjects.

An infidel or heretical king is not to be resisted, however, merely because he is an infidel or heretic.[12]

"Great indeed," says Figgis, "was the indignation evoked by the airy manner in which Bellarmine or Mariana disposed of the claims to obedience of the secular princes and fostered principles of popular sovereignty. Where the Jesuits were mistaken was in asserting that the secular power as such had no moral claim to obedience."[13]

Bellarmine admits that James I made such accusations against him. In his rebuttal he replied: "The king will not be able to prove this accusation from any of my writings. In the treatise, *De Laicis,* I have taught, at great length, that subjects must obey the laws of temporal kings, not only of necessity, but also in conscience."[14]

"Since the rulers have power from God to rule, certainly they who do not obey offend not only the ruler, but also God. They who resist the ruler resist the ordinance of God. They certainly sin in conscience who do not obey just commands. For if rulers are ministers of God and if they are to be obeyed for the love of God, certainly they offend the majesty of God who do not observe the laws of the ruler."[15]

Neither does Suarez, another Jesuit and contemporary of Cardinal Bellarmine, minimize the binding power of civil laws. "It is the Catholic and common opinion and almost a matter of faith," he says, "that human civil laws have the power of binding in conscience."[16]

Subjects have an obligation in conscience to obey the just laws of a

---

[10] *European Civilization,* ch. 54.

[11] *De Laicis,* Cap. X.

[12] *De Potest. Papae in Temp.* Cap. XX.

[13] Figgis, *Divine Right of Kings,* p. 204.

[14] From Cardinal Bellarmine's first response to King James I, but addressed to "Rudulpho II Imp. Caesari semper Augusto" Ch. III.

[15] *Supplement to De Laicis,* Cap. X, Par. 7.

[16] "Dicendum vero est legem humanam civilem habere vim et efficaciam obligandi in conscientia. Haec est sententia communis Catholicorum et videtur assertio vel de fide vel proxima fidei." *De Legibus,* iii, 21, 5.

legitimate government, but civil liberty still reserves the right to resist laws detrimental to the civic body.

While insisting upon rightful obedience, respect and reverence for king, government, and law, Bellarmine feared not to define the obligations of kings, and to outline the liberties, dignity and equality, which are the natural birthright of every citizen of the realm.

"Kings," he declares, "will profit much to remember that the people over whom they rule are of the same kind and equality as they themselves. It is possible that not a few of their subjects be more prudent, capable, conscientious, and worthy of the crown than they themselves.[17]

"Kings must not grow insolent or condemn private men; but they should carry their scepter, not in pride, but as a cross. A king ought not raise himself in pride over his subjects. Because he sits on a higher throne, he often imagines himself more excellent by nature. Thus Alexander the Great thought himself to be an immortal god, the son of Jupiter, and not the son of Philip, King of Macedonia. Death soon revealed to him who he was. The Roman Emperors, Caius and Domitian, labored under the same exaggerated idea. A king must remember that although he sits while others stand and bow, that though he rules and commands while others obey, this is not due to his merit but to the grace of God."[18]

In the seventh chapter of *De Laicis* the Cardinal writes: "Men are born equal not in wisdom or grace or qualification, but they are equal in their fundamental nature and as human beings. From this equality we correctly conclude that no man has a right to dominate or tyrannize his fellow men. Man dominates over beasts, he rules the fishes of the sea, the birds of the air, and other animals by despotic rule, but his fellow men he merely governs or directs politically." He quotes St. Augustine as saying: "*Rex—king* is derived from *regere—dirigere—to direct—to counsel;* not from *regnare* or *dominare,* to *dominate* or *lord over* with an air of proprietorship. In this sense Abraham, Isaac, Jacob, might be called kings. Therefore, our Lord warns His apostles not to dominate or lord it over the people as some of the kings of the nations lorded it over their subjects."[19] Again, he quotes St. Gregory as saying: "It is revolting to nature to raise one's self above others or to desire to be feared by one's equals."[20]

"To be ruled by a superior is not contrary, however, to human liberty, dignity, and equality. Only the despot offends thus. God did not create many men at once but only one, and from this one descended others, to indicate what kind of order and precedence He expected. Political power would be necessary even if man had not sinned; for even then he should have been a

---

[17] Utilissimum Principibus esse potest, si serio, et saepe considerent, se dominari, et praeesse hominibus ejusdem speciei, cujus ipsi sunt; et fieri posse, ut non pauci subditorum sint prudentiores, et sanctiores, et Imperio digniores, quam ipsi sint. Cap. XXII, *De Officio Principis.*

[18] Ibid.

[19] Luke 22: 25-26; Matthew 20:25; Dominare-Katakurieusin.

[20] *De Laicis,* Cap. VII.

social and civil animal and would have needed leadership. Even in the state of innocence, there would have been political subjection, there would have been a difference of sexes, faculties and power; therefore, an order of precedence and subjection. Among the angels there is a hierarchy of the order with precedence and succession; why not among men? Therefore, it is not contrary to the liberty, nor humiliating to the dignity of man to be ruled by legitimate superiors."[21]

"There is a difference between political subjection and servile subjection. In servile subjection one works for another; in political subjection one works for himself. The servant is ruled for the benefit of the master; the citizen for his own benefit. A political head seeks not his own but the people's good; otherwise, he is a tyrant. If, then, there be a question of servitude in the matter of political organization, the presiding officer is more servant than the subject. "He that will be first among you, shall be your servant."[22]

"Thus St. Gregory the Great called himself the servant of servants. Succeeding pontiffs imitated him and bishops call themselves the servants of the people."[23]

The ruler must also provide such just laws as are consonant with true liberty. "Human liberty," he says, "really consists in this, that one is free to choose the good and reject the evil. Therefore a just law does not curtail liberty; for, it does not prohibit the choosing of good and the rejection of evil, but it rather promotes the exercise of this power. The Divine law does not interfere with true liberty because it is good, therefore, a human law when good and just does not interfere with true liberty."[24]

Enumerating the virtues necessary in a ruler, Bellarmine gives the first place to fraternal charity, "for the exercise of which," he says, "prudence, justice, fortitude, and temperance are also required. Charity marks the difference between a regent and a tyrant. A good ruler will regard his subjects as children, not as servants; as brethren, not as strangers. He will not burden them with exorbitant taxes. Constantius imposed very reasonable taxes and was greatly beloved. He but signified his wants and obtained all he needed. The love and loyalty of his people were his treasure. The poor should engage a king's special care. He should be interested in the spiritual, intellectual, and physical welfare of his people."[25]

"The virtue of prudence in a king will give the proper direction to his efforts and will apply the best means of obtaining results. It is as necessary in the ruler as is obedience in the subject for the maintenance of order. Hence David enjoined his son, Solomon, to pray for the virtue of prudence as most necessary, not only for the government of others but for the

---

[21] *De Laicis*, Cap. VII.

[22] Matthew 20:27.

[23] *De Officio Principis*, Cap. XXII; *De Laicis*, Cap. VII.

[24] *De Laicis*, Cap. X.

[25] *De Officio Principis*, Cap. VII.

government and control of himself."[26]

"Justice in a ruler is that virtue which observes all laws and constitutions of the land. Alongside it, iniquity cannot abide. Rulers are to their subjects not only what the head is to the members of the body, what a shepherd is to his sheep, but they are, in a certain sense, terrestrial gods. They are mirrors into which subjects will gaze for the adjustment of their own lives. Princes should, therefore, be just, pure, sober, honorable, noble. Unless they possess these virtues, how will they correct others?"[27]

"Justice is also that virtue which distributes the rewards and honors according to merit and capacity without respect of person. In this distribution rulers and governments are often dishonest and unjust. They favor friends or relatives rather than more deserving and abler men in the state. In the punishment of offenders, justice must also be exercised according to guilt and irrespective of person in order that crime may be suppressed, peace and order maintained. The rigor of justice is not contrary to gentleness and mercy unless it proceeds from a vindictive heart and a cruel spirit. Justice and mercy are so intimately connected that they might be called devoted sisters."[28]

"Fortitude is that cardinal virtue which resists pain and overcomes all obstacles impeding the accomplishment of a certain good work. It is a virtue that is necessary in every patriotic and loyal citizen in time of peace and in the trials of war but especially in the ruler. He must not neglect the duties of his office to pursue private pleasure. A ruler who has at heart the welfare of his people in the exercise of his governing powers will lie awake whole nights devising means and ways of avoiding impending evils and of bringing about needed reforms."[29]

"The virtue of temperance will restrain a ruler and moderate all his actions and activities, his rewards and his punishments, his laws and precepts. He will be patient and enduring in giving ear to the complaints and miseries of his subjects. He will listen to counsel though he reserves his judgment. He will cultivate a refinement of spirit and manner which bespeaks the self-control and poise which so well adorns and becomes the dignity and majesty of the ruler."[30]

Recalling the several democratic principles of Cardinal Bellarmine as noted in this chapter, our attention and admiration are again drawn to the well-balanced middle course pursued in his political theories. He is not a revolutionist, who would lightly question the good judgment of a ruler or subvert his authority.

He commands obedience in conscience to all civil laws that are not certainly detrimental to the commonweal. He does not cringe, however,

---

[26] Ibid., Cap. VIII.

[27] Ibid., Cap. IX.

[28] *De Officio Principis,* Cap. X.

[29] Ibid., Cap. XI.

[30] Ibid., Cap. XII.

before the servile theory of passive obedience and nonresistance. Patriotism and loyalty, respect and obedience for civil authority, as well as the dignity, rights, liberties, and human equality of every citizen found a staunch protagonist in Cardinal Bellarmine.

If democracy is a government primarily for the people; if it is conscious of the dignity and equality of every man as a human being; if it recognizes the rights and liberties of the private citizen; then again the defense of these principles by Cardinal Bellarmine is another proof that the Christian Church, while upholding rightful civil obedience and loyalty did not oppose but rather defend and promote the just rights and liberties of the common people.

CHAPTER VIII
RELIGIOUS FREEDOM

The fundamental concern of man's life is his religion. The religious needs and obligations of man are the source of the most sacred rights and liberties conceivable in life. For that reason, the fiercest of all strifes are religious strifes, and the most sanguinary of all wars are religious wars. One of the guarantees of true democracy is freedom of religion from state control. Religious liberty has its root in political and civil liberty. Under the head of religious freedom, we are here understanding freedom from lay or state interference in the work proper to the sphere of the Church as a religious organization of direct and divine institution.

In the history of religious freedom, three stages are sometimes noted. In the first stage, in ancient times, the state prescribed a religion of its own, which all subjects were forced to embrace. The Roman Emperor was also the *Summus Pontifex.* It was the era of religious subjection. Before the conversion of Constantine, the Christian Church was regarded as an enemy of the state, an enemy to be exterminated.

In the second stage the Church labored to impress this concept of her independence as a spiritual society upon the state. Conscious of her divine institution and commission, the Church refused to recognize any authority of the civil rulers in spiritual matters.

The state gradually realized its incompetence to decide upon questions of religion, and the claim of the Church as a distinct spiritual authority was recognized in the mediaeval world. This era was ushered in by the conversion of Constantine, and amid the vicissitudes of conflict between temporal and spiritual heads—as we witnessed it particularly in the long drawn out investiture struggle—continued through the Middle Ages.

In this period the Church was never entirely free from lay and temporal interference even in spiritual affairs. Mediaeval government recognized, however, that the practice of the true religion of God was necessary to the well-being of the state. At the same time it was convinced of the unity and truth of the Christian religion.

It regarded as revolutionary and traitorous any defection from that established true faith, and so punished heresy as an act of treason to the State and as dangerous to its well-being. According to mediaeval political principle, as repeated by Cardinal Bellarmine, the foreigner, or non-Christian, not being a citizen of this Christian state, was not amenable to the laws of the state.

The third stage is that of complete religious independence and freedom for all forms of belief, at least in principle, such as we see it in many lands today. This third stage or concept of religious liberty does not distinguish between true and false religions, nor does it presume to decide which religion is true. It proposes to grant equal protection to all religions, on the plea that religious conviction is a matter of conscience and good faith before God.

One essential element and ideal in the doctrine and organization of the Christian religion is unity. There should be but one fold and one shepherd "Freedom will be most complete where unity exists as the triumph of truth and not of force."[1]

Christianity professes to teach a true religion or relation to God; but true religion cannot harbor within itself contradictory elements or religious doctrines or sects. Contrary to this fundamental Christian constitution, some kings seemed not to distinguish between politico-national aspirations and the Christian ideal of one Catholic or universal Church. To develop national states in the sixteenth century it seemed necessary to organize national churches independent of the Pope, hitherto the center of unity.

Divine right theory made the king vicar also of Christ the Priest; and since the authority of the Pope was to be banished, it was convenient for the king to arrogate to himself, as presumed vicar of Christ the Priest, the power and right of prescribing the religion of his subjects.

The doctrine of "passive obedience," of "non-resistance," principles like "the king can do no wrong...he who possesses the land prescribes the religion," logically infringed upon the religious convictions of men. In the German Palatinate the religion was changed four times in sixty years. To establish such tyranny over the consciences of men, the League of Smalcald was formed in 1530. In Germany fierce conflicts raged for liberty of conscience between the "Evangelical Union," composed of Lutherans and Calvinists on the one side and the "Catholic League" on the other. In 1618 began the fratricidal struggle which is known as the Thirty Years' War.

Throughout the Middle Ages, the Church had struggled to free itself from state and lay interference. In the sixteenth century divine right theorists would again return the world to the time of the Roman Caesars when the emperor was *Summus Pontifex.*

"The Zwinglian system blended state and Church in a single organization."[2] The government of Zurich took to itself the regulation of worship. In Calvin's code, civil government prescribed the frequency and form of church services. All deviations entailed fines. Visitation and search of homes was instituted to punish infractions of the code. The notion of liberty whether civil or religious, was hateful to Luther's despotic nature, and contrary to his interpretation of Scripture.

On the question of the state's right in the Church, Cardinal Bellarmine wrote: "Some would have kings to be not only protectors and defenders of religion but they would also make them judges and teachers. As foremost members of the Church they would have them decide controversies of faith, to preside at general Church councils, and to appoint ministers and pastors. Kings, we admit, hold a first place among Christians; but they hold no place in the inner household of the Church. In the Church the first place is held by the supreme pontiff and bishops; the second place by the priests; the third place by the deacons and other clerics; the last place is held by the laity among whom are also numbered the kings and princes." He quotes the letter

---

[1] Acton, *History of Freedom,* p. 152.

[2] Dunning, *From Luther to Montesquieu,* p. 25.

of Pope Gelasius to the Emperor Anastasius: " 'Know, most gentle son, that although you preside in worldly dignity, you bow your head to the ministers of God.' Christ committed the Church to St. Peter and the bishops, not to Tiberius and his prefects. For three hundred years the Church was well governed solely by bishops and priests without any assistance from Christian princes."[3]

In 1606 a great conflict which involved the question of Church and State rights, arose between England's King James I and his theologians on the one side, and Bellarmine and Suarez on the side of the Church. James had oppressed Catholic subjects severely and imposed on them heavy money fines on account of their religious profession. He demanded of them an oath of allegiance, skilfully devised by the apostate Perkins, that contained an act of renunciation of their spiritual allegiance to the Pope, and made every subject declare that the international authority, exercised by Popes from Gregory VII to Boniface VIII, was not only incorrect but heretical. Recusants (those who refused to attend the state church), were threatened with imprisonment and several priests were condemned to the scaffold.

In his pamphlet of 1607 King James attacked Bellarmine in particular, because of the letter he had written to the English Archpriest Blackwell, in which Bellarmine declared the oath unlawful, and in a most inspiring and consoling manner encouraged Blackwell to persevere in fidelity to God and his Church. This letter had fallen into the hands of James and in 1608 he issued a treatise in defense of the oath of allegiance entitled, *Triplici Nodo Triplex Cuneus.* Bellarmine replied in his *Responsio Matthaei Torti.* The king concealed his name in this treatise as he thought it beneath his dignity to contend openly with a man whose family lineage was no better than that of his meanest subject.

In his second attack James did not conceal his name. In 1609 Bellarmine replied also in his own name and dedicated this *Apologia* to the "Emperor Rudolph II and to all kings and princes who acknowledge God as their Father and the Catholic Church as their Mother." Concerning the impropriety on the part of the king to contend with so lowly a person as Bellarmine, the Cardinal remarked: "I cannot see the necessity, in a theological discussion, of one side's having as many titled uncles as the other, so long as both possess equal knowledge." [4] "Christian subjects," he declared, "owe obedience for conscience' sake to infidel rulers in those things which are not contrary to the law of God. (But) In that oath of fidelity (to King James I) there was contained not only a test of civil obedience, but an abjuration of the Pope's power of binding and loosing in spiritualities."[5]

The oath of allegiance, while it was an oath of fidelity to the king, was at the same time an oath of disobedience to the spiritual authority of the Pope. For this reason Pope Clement VIII warned the English Catholics not to take this oath. They could have taken it, had it contained nothing more than an

---

[3] *De Laicis,* Cap. XVII.

[4] *Apologia,* (Rudolpho II), Cap. IV.

[5] Ibid., Cap. VI.

oath of fidelity to the king. "We admonish the English Catholics to serve and obey their earthly king as long as he does not command anything displeasing to the Heavenly King."[6]

We must bear in mind that Henry VIII, Edward VI, Elizabeth and James I set themselves up as spiritual heads of the national church as well as of the state. "The royal dignity," said James, "is at once civil and ecclesiastical; the king is not a simple laic as the papists, ana-baptists and puritans fancy in their dreams."[7]

He endeavored to support his claim to spiritual authority by texts like these: "Wherefore be subject of necessity, not only for wrath, but also for conscience' sake" (Romans 13:5); "Be subject to every human creature for God's sake whether it be to the king as excelling, or to governors as sent by Him for the punishment of evildoers" (I Peter 2: 13-14).

Bellarmine explained that "these and similar texts all referred to pagan rulers for there were no others in the time of Christ and the Apostles. But no one will say that these pagan rulers had any spiritual authority in the Church."[8]

"If the laity have authority in the Church," he argued, "they have it from themselves or from another; they have it not from themselves, for spiritual authority is not a natural right but a divine, positive, and supernatural prerogative; they have it not from another, for Christ said to St. Peter in particular, 'Feed my sheep.'"[9]

'The Holy Ghost hath placed you bishops, to rule the Church of God'" (Acts 20: 28). He quotes St. Martin of Tours as telling the Emperor openly that he was "in the Church but not over the Church". He cites the examples of Valentinian, Theodosius, Basilius, Theodoric, Charlemagne, as rulers who did not venture to interfere in affairs of Churches.[10] "It pertains to the Church of God and not to the king to bind the consciences of men. Only to the Church was it spoken, 'Whatsoever thou shalt bind on earth shall be bound in Heaven.'"[11]

"To the great Catholic antagonists of King James, especially to Bellarmine and Suarez," says Alfred O'Rahilly, "the world owes a real debt for their triumphant vindication of conscience and law."[12]

One phase of the struggle for religious liberty consisted in the attempted abolition by divine right theorists of the ancient tradition of clerical

---

[6] Ibid., Cap. XV.

[7] *Basilicon Doron* (Frankfort, 1632) p. 71.

[8] *Pro Juramento Fidelitatis.*

[9] John 21:16-17.

[10] *Pro Juramento Fidelitatis.*

[11] *Pro Juramento Fidelitatis.*

[12] "Suarez and Democracy," *Studies,* March, 1918.

exemption and immunity from civil jurisdiction.[13]

As strong monarchs arose they encroached more and more on the rights and prerogatives of Church and clerics. In 1164 England reduced the power of ecclesiastical courts. In 1179 no property might be bestowed upon the Church without royal permission. In 1392 appeals to Rome had been forbidden.

In France, Philip the Fair, taught by his jurists that the possessions of his subjects belonged to him, and always in need of subsidies, took the possessions of the Knights Templars, of the Jews, of all taxpayers, and disregarding the traditional right of ecclesiastical immunity, laid his hands on the possessions of the Church, although the Church had, in spite of her rightful immunities, always contributed to the public expenses by voluntary donations. It has been estimated that the French clergy in the last half of the thirteenth century contributed one-fifth of all its possessions to the king.

"By confiscation of Church lands and control of the clergy, in the sixteenth century," says Hayes, "the Tudor Sovereigns in England, the kings in Scandinavia, and the German princes were personally enriched and freed from fear of being hampered in absolute tendencies by an independent ecclesiastical organization."[14]

The question of clerical exemption became an open and acute one about the year 1606 in the controversy of the Republic of Venice with the Papacy. Ancient privileges of Church and clergy were abolished. It was declared to be unlawful for the Church to own or buy real estate or to accept any gifts. The clergy were subjected to civil courts.

During the Pontificate of Paul V the Doge enacted laws concerning the erection of ecclesiastical institutions and pious endowments. Two clerics were arraigned before the civil courts. Pope Paul demanded the abrogation of such laws and the release of the clerics. He finally placed Venice under interdict.

Among the many controversial pamphlets that followed between the Pope and the Republic, those of Bellarmine on the side of the Church occupied a prominent place. These pamphlets were published in Rome in 1606. In March of 1607 the laws were suspended and the clerics released. Paul V then lifted the interdict.

Ecclesiastical freedom rests upon the Scriptural doctrine that the ministers of the Church are vested with spiritual authority, not by any consent or acclamation of the people, but by the ordination of ministers as committed to the apostles by Christ, the Son of God.

Clerical immunity was founded on such Scriptural texts which declared the priest or cleric as taken from "among men and ordained for men in the

---

[13] Clerical Immunity, as recognized in the Middle Ages, exempted the clergy from secular jurisdiction, from temporal lawsuits, whether criminal or civil. In temporal as well as spiritual indictments, he was subject exclusively to the jurisdiction of the ecclesiastical judges.

[14] Carlton J.H. Hayes, *Political and Social History of Modern Europe*, vol. I, p. 168.

things that pertain to God."[15]

If the whole life of the cleric is dedicated to the service of men, why should an additional tax be levied upon him? "If the cleric is taken from the world and consecrated to God, why should aught thus given be withdrawn?"[16] Again, the cleric is the ambassador for Christ, the minister of God; how can a secular court presume to judge God's anointed representative?

In his twenty-eighth chapter on Clerics, Bellarmine lays down the following principles in explanation and proof of clerical exemption as viewed in his time:

First: "In ecclesiastical cases clerics are free by divine right from the secular powers." By "divine right" he understands not a direct precept, but a deduction from the Old or the New Testament. In proof of this principle he cites the example of the apostles, ecclesiastical writers, and the Church Councils.

Second: "Clerics are not exempt from the observance of civil laws which are not opposed to the Sacred Canons or the clerical state. For clerics are also citizens of the state and as such they should live according to the laws of the state. If the government, e. g., sets a fixed price on certain articles, prohibits the export of produce, forbids the carrying of arms, or travel without lights by night, clerics are bound to observe such laws."

Third: "Clerics cannot be judged by secular courts even though they transgress against the civil law, but their case should be referred to an ecclesiastical judge. The codes of Theodosius and Valentinian, also the Justinian Code, prescribed that clerics be referred to their bishops for trial unless previously despoiled of their dignity."

Fourth: "The goods of clerics and of the Church, are free from taxation by secular princes. The custom of all nations in all times sanctioned such a practice. Among the Hebrews, the Levites were free from tributes. Among the Egyptians under Pharaoh, priests were exempt.[17] The same customs prevailed among the Gentile priests according to Aristotle."

Fifth: "The exemption of clerics in political affairs of both person and goods was introduced by human and by divine right. Nearly all theologians and canonists held that clerics were exempt by the law of nations or *Jus Gentium,* which, according to Bellarmine, partakes both of the natural and of the positive law of nations."

The Church of Christ has a God-given mission and duty. Consequently the Church has God-given powers, jurisdiction, independence, prerogatives and rights in its own sphere which can not rightly be infringed upon by the State. The Church unfolds its greatest blessings when it labors unhampered by lay or state interference and dictation.

Cardinal Bellarmine fearlessly denied the king or prince any right to act as judge, teacher, presiding officer or governor in the Church. To dictate or to

---

[15] St. Paul, Hebrews 5:1.

[16] *De Clericis,* Cap. XXVIII.

[17] Genesis XLVII: 26.

change the religion of subjects, to infringe upon the consciences of men, the Cardinal claimed to be beyond the sphere of the secular power.

He asserted the right of the Church to acquire and own such properties as were necessary and useful to promote the blessings of religion among men. Freedom from taxation of church property he defended as an ancient and well recognized ecclesiastical exemption. While making these claims, he amply proved against King James I that loyalty to Church involves no disloyalty to Country. These are principles of relation between church and state which all fair-minded men of modern times uphold.

"To the labors of the opponents of divine right," among whom Cardinal Bellarmine was the foremost, "we owe it," says Figgis, "that liberty of thought has become a recognized principle of modern life." [18]

---

[18] *Divine Right of Kings,* p. 216.

CONCLUSION

The Middle Ages have been branded as autocratic; the Catholicism of that age as retarding the progress of mankind and restricting the blessings of liberty and democracy. Democracy has been styled the "Child of the Reformation." In the foregoing chapters we have endeavored to demonstrate from the original writings of one of the foremost Catholic churchmen at the beginning of the modern period and from the testimony of unbiased historians that the true sources of democracy lie in the institutions and doctrines of the Catholic Church.

Out of the foregoing chapters we must gather the conclusion that at a time when royal heads were tracing the origin of their power from the Olympic heights of divine appointment, when as a sacred and royal caste they set themselves apart from and above the rest of mankind, when they were no longer content to deck their brows with the crown of temporal power but coveted likewise the tiara of spiritual supremacy, when civil liberty, human equality, and religious freedom were being tramped in the dust, there stepped out before the despotic court of that day, with something of dramatic vigor and majesty, like another John the Baptist or an Ambrose, this staunch and fearless Cardinal of the ancient Church, in unfaltering terms defining the foundations of democracy, the obligations of kings and subjects, the principles of civil liberty, human dignity, and equality.

While men, thus far, have been unwilling to proclaim any particular form of government as perfect, whether in theory or practice, a refined and highly developed form of democracy seems to approach nearest their political ideal. Any form of government may descend to tyranny and no form of good government is necessarily inconsistent with true liberty.

The Church, too, has never found it necessary or advisable to make any definite or official pronouncement on this subject. She has merely lent her support and cooperation, at all times, to any good government competent to procure for mankind the greatest amount of general welfare. In the eighth century she looked to Charlemagne and she strengthened kings to reconstruct a shattered world.

Later on in the Middle Ages when monarchy exceeded its limits, the Church opposed it and promoted popular institutions. In the sixteenth century when autocracy waxed boldest, representative Churchmen like Cardinal Bellarmine, Suarez, Mariana, Molina, Robert Persons, Toletus, Bannez, Gregory of Valentia, increased their protest against the insolence of kings and defended the mediaeval institutions of liberty and rights of people and Church.

That all power, civil as well as ecclesiastical, is derived from God, is an undeniable doctrine of Christianity. But the manner in which political power is vested in a ruler is a question open to discussion. In his Encyclical, *Immortale Dei,* the Pope, Leo XIII, asserts that "the right to rule is not necessarily bound up with any special mode of government," and that "it may take this or that form provided it insure the general welfare."

The political philosophy of Cardinal Bellarmine reflects in most instances, however, the general mind of the Catholic Church, and his opinion is that of the majority of the best Catholic theologians and political thinkers. Suarez, another staunch defender of popular sovereignty in those days, proved by a long list of theological and canonical authorities, such as Cajetan, Victoria, Soto, Molina, and St. Thomas Aquinas, that the political doctrine of Cardinal Bellarmine was the ancient, commonly accepted and true teaching.

Alfred O'Rahilly makes the statement: "I have made the laborious investigation of every accessible Catholic philosopher and theologian from the thirteenth to the nineteenth century and here is the significant result: Fifty-two writers prior to Suarez and eighty-seven after him, uphold the principle that government is based upon the consent of the governed; sixty-five do not discuss the subject at all, and only seven Gallicans of very doubtful orthodoxy, reject the principle."[1]

The idea of sovereignty as directly committed by God to the people, and by them conferred upon some one or some few for their common weal, was indicated even by Aristotle; it was outlined more definitely by St. Thomas,[2] and more fully developed and freely taught in the Dominican and Jesuit schools from the middle of the sixteenth century.

It is worthy of note how literally the thoughts of this great Cardinal of the Catholic Church have been translated into our American Constitution. Alfred O'Rahilly, an eminent scholar and writer in political science, believes that Bellarmine's doctrine, as quoted by Robert Filmer in his *Patriarcha*, though for purposes of refutation, influenced George Mason in writing the Virginia Declaration of Rights, and Jefferson in drafting the Declaration of Independence. "The Declaration of Independence," he states, "is an accurate transcript of the Catholic mind."[3]

"As in England so in America the stream of Catholic democratic influence which began as a rivulet, perceptible here and there in phrase or reference, ends by becoming a broad river of accepted commonplaces. There is strong historical evidence, that it is to the great Jesuit antagonists of James I (Bellarmine and Suarez), that England and America primarily owe the conception of democratic government. There is not a single English democratic writer between the Reformation and Suarez. The seventeenth century witnessed a reaction against the Protestant theory and practice of despotism by divine right, and a return, partially at least, to the mediaeval ideas of natural rights, popular sovereignty, liberties of municipal and corporate bodies. The twentieth century is manifesting a further readoption of those political ideas."[4]

Mr. Gaillard Hunt of the Library of Congress shows in a very interesting and enlightening article in the *Catholic Historical Review*, October, 1917,

---

[1] "Theology on Tyranny," *Irish Theological Quarterly*, Jan. 1921.

[2] Cf. *St. Thomas' Political Doctrine and Democracy*, by Rev. Edward Murphy (1921).

[3] "Sources of English and American Democracy," *Studies*, March, 1918.

[4] "Catholic Origin of Democracy," *Studies*, March, 1919.

that perhaps the immediate source of that part of the (Virginia) Declaration of Rights and of the Declaration of Independence, which proclaimed the equality of man and sovereignty by consent of the people, is to be found in the political theories of this same Cardinal Bellarmine.

In 1776, he relates, men were discussing the problem of how far they might enjoy their natural freedom and at the same time submit to good government; what were the rights and duties of governors and the governed? While George Mason and Thomas Jefferson had the classical literature of Athens and Rome at their command, and well understood those states, their immediate inspiration came from more modern sources.

The names of Montesquieu, Rousseau, and James Berg are often mentioned as possibly having influenced the spirit and contents of our American Declaration. The *Spirit of Laws* by Montesquieu, though read in America, did not present that theory of government, which was sought by the Fathers of our Country. Rousseau's writings were less widely known than Montesquieu's. George Mason, not knowing French, in all probability never read the *Contrat Social*, nor had Rousseau's writings obtained currency in Virginia in 1776. The book of James Berg appeared in 1775, rather too late to have rendered service in May of 1776, even if it had discussed such general principles as are laid down in these two American Declarations.

Writings that may have had some influence in crystallizing the American idea of democratic government were those of Sidney and Locke.

A treatise on government that was very popular, much read and discussed among Americans in 1776, was that of Algernon Sidney. Now Sidney's discourses on government were a refutation of Robert Filmer's *Patriarcha* which in turn was a refutation of Cardinal Bellarmine's theory on popular sovereignty against divine right. Sidney had been put to death in England in 1683 for his alleged writings against the divine right theory and in the mind of Americans he was a hero.

Another treatise on government, as widely read but not quite so popular nor interesting as Algernon Sidney's work, was John Locke's *Two Treatises on Government* which appeared in 1690. Like Sidney, Locke wrote in reply to Filmer. Locke himself states, on the title page, that in his two treatises "the false principles and foundation of Sir Robert Filmer and his followers are detected and overthrown;" that Filmer's "system is no more but this: 'That all government is absolute monarchy' and the ground he builds on is this, 'that no man is born free.'"

Giving his own views, Locke wrote, "Men being, as has been said, by nature all free, equal, and independent, no one can be put out of this estate, and subjected to the political power of another, without his own consent."[5] "The greater part of the political ideas of Milton, Locke, and Rousseau may be found in the ponderous Latin of Jesuits," says Lord Acton.[6]

This Robert Filmer against whom Sidney and Locke had so much to say, was the private theologian of James I and the chief exponent of the divine

---

[5] *Works*, edition of 1824, Vol. IV, p. 394.

[6] Acton, *History of Freedom*, p. 82.

right theory. His *Patriarcha* was written for the express purpose of refuting Cardinal Bellarmine's political theories on popular sovereignty. The opening page of *Patriarcha* epitomized Cardinal Bellarmine's doctrine. The first sentence of the book reads:

"Since the time that School-Divinity began to flourish there hath been a common opinion maintained, as well by Divines, as by divers other Learned Men, which affirms: 'Mankind is naturally endowed and born with Freedom from all Subjection, and at liberty to choose what Form of Government it please: And that the Power which any one Man hath over others, was at first bestowed according to the discretion of the Multitude.'

"This tenet First hatched In the schools and hath been fostered by all succeeding papists for good divinity. The Divines also of the Reformed Churches have entertained it, and the Common People everywhere tenderly embrace it, as being most plausible to Flesh and Blood, for that it prodigally distributes a Portion of Liberty to the meanest of the Multitude who magnifie Liberty, as if the height of Human Felicity were only to be found in it, never remembering that the desire of Liberty was the first cause of the Fall of Adam."

On the fourth page of *Patriarcha* we read:

"To make evident the Grounds of this Question, about the Natural Liberty of Mankind, I will lay down some passages of Cardinal Bellarmine, that may best unfold the State of this controversie. Secular or Civil Power (saith he) is instituted by men; It is in the people, unless they bestow it on a Prince. This Power is immediately in the whole Multitude, as in the subject of it; for this Power is in Divine Law, but the Divine Law hath given this power to no particular man. If the Positive Law be taken away, there is left no Reason why amongst a Multitude (who are Equal) one rather than another should bear Rule over the Rest. Power is given by the multitude to one man, or to more, by the same Law of Nature; for the Commonwealth cannot exercise this Power, therefore it is bound to bestow it upon some One man or some Few. It depends upon the Consent of the multitude to ordain over themselves a King, Counsel or other Magistrates; and if there be a lawful cause the multitude may change the Kingdom into an Aristocracy or Democracy. Thus far Bellarmine; in which passages are comprised the strength of all that I have read or heard produced for the Natural Liberty of the Subject."[7]

The opening sentence of Sidney's discourses ran:

"Having lately seen a book entitled *Patriarcha* written by Sir Robert Filmer concerning the universal and undistinguished right of all kings, I thought a time of leisure might well be employed in examining his doctrine and the questions arising from it: which seem so far to concern all mankind."

Commenting on the quotation in *Patriarcha* from Cardinal Bellarmine, Sidney remarked of Filmer:

"He absurdly imputes to the School Divines that which was taken up by them as a common notion, written in the heart of every man, denied by none, but such as were degenerated into beasts. The school men could not lay more

---

[7] Cf. De Laicis, Cap. VI, Notes 1, 2, 3, and Cap. III, of this dissertation, Notes 22, 23, and 24.

approved foundations than that man is naturally free; that he cannot justly be deprived of that liberty without cause; that only those governments can be called just which are established by the consent of nations."

Americans revered both the name and the writings of Algernon Sidney. They liked to associate themselves with him. They named their children and their country places "Sidney." His "noble book," as it was styled, could be found in every large library in 1776. Every reading man had read it in part or in whole. An American edition of his works was published in Philadelphia as late as 1804. Now the argument of this "noble book" of Sidney's and of Locke's two treatises revolved about *Patriarcha's* denunciation of Bellarmine's democratic theory.

George Mason, Thomas Jefferson, James Madison, the framers and builders of our American Constitution and Republic, could not have been ignorant of Sidney, Locke, Filmer, and Bellarmine. "Locke and Sidney," says Dr. Figgis, "if they did not take their political faith bodily from Suarez or Bellarmine, managed in a remarkable degree to conceal the difference between the two." [8]

While the catalogue of George Mason's library has not survived, we do know that Thomas Jefferson, drafter of the Declaration of Independence, possessed a copy of *Patriarcha* in his library and also a handsome folio of 497 pages of the discourses of Algernon Sidney. If he read but the opening pages of Sidney's and Filmer's books, he had the principles of democracy as propounded by Bellarmine, in a nutshell. It is more than likely, however, that the curiosity of Jefferson and Mason prompted them to look more deeply into the original writings of this Catholic Schoolman.

They had not far to go. In the library of Princeton University there was a copy of Cardinal Bellarmine's works. James Madison, a member of the committee which framed the Virginia Declaration of Rights, was a graduate of Princeton. Probably he read Bellarmine, for at this period of his life he read everything he could lay his hands on and was deeply versed in religious controversy. There were copies of some of Bellarmine's books in Virginia too, probably at the Episcopal High School near Alexandria.

It might be remarked that several members of the committee which drew up the Declaration of Rights had been educated in England, where the writings of Bellarmine were not unpopular even among those who were most inimical to his faith. "In all probability," says Figgis, "the name of either the Pope or Bellarmine will be prominent on the first page of any tract or pamphlet in behalf of royal rights written during the seventeenth century." [9]

"Filmer was better known to laymen in America than Bellarmine," says Gaillard Hunt. "Nothing which Filmer wrote himself, however, had any influence upon Mason and Jefferson. He was a dead author and his doctrine had no interest for men who were convinced of the equal rights of men; but the quotation he gave from Bellarmine and his epitome of Bellarmine's doctrine seems to have lodged in their memory, to reappear in a new form in

[8] *Trans. Royal Hist. Society,* XI, (1897), p. 4.

[9] *Divine Right of Kings,* p. 177.

the Declarations which they wrote. Neither in Sidney nor in Locke nor in the writings of any other author with whom they were familiar is there as complete an epitome of the doctrine they announced."

In the light of these facts, let us compare a few excerpts from the writings of Cardinal Bellarmine, from Filmer's quotations from him, from Sidney's noble book, from Mason's Virginia Declaration of Rights (Vir. Decl. R.) and Jefferson's Declaration of Independence (Decl. of Ind.), which reveal striking similarities.

Bellarmine: (literal translation): "Political power emanates from God. Government was introduced by divine law but the divine law has given this power to no particular man. *De Laicis*, Cap. VI, 1.

Bellarmine: (as quoted by Filmer) "This power is in the divine law, but the divine law has given this power to no particular man." p. 4.

Vir. Decl. R.: "That power is by GOD and NATURE vested in the people."

Decl. of Ind.: "They (the people) are endowed by their creator with certain unalienable rights."

Bellarmine: "Men must be governed by some one, lest they be willing to perish. It is impossible for men to live together without some one to care for the common good. Society must have power to protect and preserve itself." *De Laicis*, Cap. VI, Notes 1 and 2.

Vir. Decl. R.: "Government is or ought to be instituted for the common benefit, protection and security of the people, nation or community."

Decl. of Ind.: 'To secure these rights (Life, Liberty and the pursuit of Happiness) governments are instituted among men."

Bellarmine: "This power is immediately as in its subject, in the whole multitude." Ch. VI, Note 2. "The people themselves, immediately and directly, hold the political power so long as they have not transferred this power to some king or ruler." *De Clericis*, Ch. VII. "The commonwealth cannot exercise this power itself, therefore, it is held to transfer it in some one man or some few." *De Laicis*, Ch. VI.

Bellarmine as quoted by Filmer: "This power is immediately in the whole multitude as in the subject of it. It is in the people unless they bestow it upon a Prince. The commonwealth cannot exercise this power, therefore, it is bound to bestow it upon some one man or a few."

Sidney: "If the multitude do institute, the multitude may abrogate." Edition 1763, page 15. "Only those governments can be called just which are established by the consent of the nations." Ibid., page 155. That all the power of the prince is originally in the people and derived from the people." Ibid,. pages 115-116.

Vir. Decl. R.: "All power belongs to the people."

Decl. of Ind.: "Governments are instituted among men, deriving their just powers from the consent of the governed."

Bellarmine: "In a commonwealth all men are born naturally free and equal." *De Clericis,* Ch. VII. "There is no reason why amongst equals one should rule rather than another." *De Laicis,* Ch. VI, Note 2.

Bellarmine as quoted by Filmer: "Mankind is naturally endowed and born with freedom from all subjection. There is left no reason why amongst a multitude (who are equal) one rather than another should bear rule over the rest."

Sidney: "The school men could not lay more approved foundations than that man is naturally free; that he cannot justly be deprived of that liberty without cause."

Vir. Decl. R.: "All men are born equally free and independent." This clause came from the convention with this change: "All men are BY NATURE, equally free and independent."

Decl. of Ind.: "All men are created equal."

Bellarmine: "For legitimate reason they (the people) can change the government to an aristocracy or a democracy or vice versa." *De Laicis,* Ch. VI. "It depends upon the consent of men to place over themselves a king, consul, or magistrate." *De Laicis,* Ch. VI.

Bellarmine as quoted by Filmer: "It depends upon the Consent of the multitude to ordain over themselves a King, consul or, other Magistrate; and if there be a lawful cause the multitude may change the Kingdom into an Aristocracy or a Democracy."

Sidney: "We say in general 'he that institutes may also abrogate'; if the multitude, therefore, do institute the multitude may abrogate."

Vir. Decl. R.: "When government fails to confer common benefit, a majority of the people have a right to change it."

Decl. of Ind.: "Whenever any form of government becomes destructive of these ends, it is the Right of the People to alter or abolish it, and to institute a new government.... Prudence, indeed, will dictate that governments long established should not be changed for light and transient causes."

"Were Mason and Jefferson conscious of their debt to Bellarmine?" asks Gaillard Hunt, " or did they use Filmer's presentation of his doctrine without knowing that they were doing so? Did the Americans realize that they were staking their lives, their fortunes and their sacred honor in support of a theory of government which had come down to them as announced by a Catholic priest?

We cannot answer these questions, but it should be a satisfaction to Catholics to know that the fundamental pronouncements upon which was built the greatest of modern revolts, found their best support in the writings of a Prince of the Church.

The general conclusion that must necessarily be gathered from the above chapters is that the fundamental and all-pervading idea in Blessed Cardinal Bellarmine's political philosophy, was one of popular government. He defended the world against the anarchistic tendencies of social compact theories. He encouraged obedience without servility; he upheld authority without tyranny, liberty without license, participation in government without anarchy.

The whole strength of his great intellect was thrown into the struggle to defend and to popularize the principles of self-determination and representative government which underlie every successful effort to establish real democracy in our day. He outlined the principles which a few centuries later were embodied in all modern, liberal and well-organized democratic governments.

BIBLIOGRAPHY

All scripture references are to the Douay Version of the Holy Bible

SOURCES

Bellarmini, Roberti, Opera Omnia, Neapoli, Joseph Giuleano, 1856
De Laicis
De Monarchia De Clericis
De Romani Pontificis Ecclesiastica Monarchia
De Potestate Papae in Rebus Temporalibus, adversus Guilielmum Barclaium
De Potestate Pontificis Temporali, Lib. V.
De Conciliis et Ecclesia
De Conciliorum Auctoritate
Responsio ad A pologiam Pro Juramento Fidelitatis
Risposta Del Cardinale Bellarmino al Trattato Dei Sette Teologi Di Venezia
Apologia ad Libra Jacobi
De Translatione Imperii Rontani a Graecis ad Francos DeExemption Clericorum
Appendix ad Libros de Summo Pontifice
De Officio Principis Christiani
Responsio ad Oppositiones F. Pauli Servitae et Marsilii Recognitio Librorum Omnibus Roberti Bellarmini

Suarez, Franciscus, *De Legibus ac de Deo Legislatore,* Partes 2, Neapoli, 1872
De Defensione Fidei

HISTORICAL AND CRITICAL WORKS

Acton, Lord—*Letters to Mary Gladstone,* New York, 1905. *History of Freedom,* New York, Macmillan, 1909.

Adams, G. B.—*Civilization During the Middle Ages,* New York, Scribner, 1914.

Allies, T. W.-—*The Formation of Christendom,* Cincinnati, Benziger, 1898.

Encyclopedia Americana, Americana Corporation, New York, 1922, 30 volumes.

Augustine, St.—*De Civitate Dei*, Macmillan, 1925.

Balmes, James—*European Civilization,* Baltimore, Murphy, 1850.

Barry, W. F.—*Papal Monarchy*, (from St. Gregory the Great to Boniface VIII, 590-1303), New York, G. P. Putnam's Sons, 1902.

Beard, Charles A.—*American Government and Politics*, New York, Macmillan, 1920.

Belloc, Hilaire—*Europe and the Faith*, New York, Paulist Press, 1920.

Bluntschli, J. K.—*The Theory of State*, Oxford, Clarendon Press, 1892.

Bryce, James—*Modern Democracies*, New York, Macmillan, 1921, 2 vols. *The Holy Roman Empire*, New York, Macmillan, 1907. *The American Commonwealth*, New York, Macmillan, 1910. *Studies on History and Jurisprudence*, 2 vols., New York, Oxford University Press, 1901.

Cambridge Mediaeval History, Vol. III, New York, Macmillan, 1922.

Cambridge Modern History, Vol. VI, *Reformation*, 1904, Vol. III, *The Wars of Religion*, New York, Macmillan, 1909.

Carlyle, R. W. and A. J.—*History of Mediaeval Political Theory in the West*, New York, Putnam, Vol. I, 1903; Vol. II, 1910; Vol. III, 1916; Vol. IV, 1922.

Catholic Encyclopedia, New York, Encyclopedia Press.

Cronin, N.—*The Science of Ethics*, New York, 1909.

The League of Nations Covenant, *Studies*, March, 1919.

Devivier, W.—*Christian Apologetics*, 2 vols. San Jose, Cal., Popp & Hogan, 1913.

De Vos, Julius E.—*Fifteen Hundred Years of Europe*, O'Donnell Press, Chicago, 1924.

Duchesne, L.—*Temporal Sovereignty ot the Pope*, New York.

Dunning, William A—*History of Political Theories*, 2 vols., New York, Macmillan, 1919.

Figgis, J. Neville—*The Theory of the Divine Right of Kings*, Cambridge University Press, 1896. *From Gerson to Grotius*, Cambridge, University Press, 1923.

Filmer, Robert—*Patriarcha*, in *Locke's Two Treatises of Civil Government*, London, Routledge & Sons, 1884.

Ford, Henry Jones—*Representative Government,* New York, 1924.

Galloni, P. Giuseppe, S. J.—*Il Beato Roberto Bellarmino,* Roma. 1924.

Gettell, Raymond G.—*History of Political Thought,* The Century Company, New York, 1924.

Gierke, Otto—*Political Theories of the Middle Ages,* Trans. by F. W. Maitland, Cambridge, University Press, 1900.

Gisler, Anton—*Der Modernismus,* Cincinnati, Benziger, 1912.

Gosselin, M.—*Power of the Popes during the Middle Ages,* 2 vols. Trans. Rev. M. Kelley, Baltimore, Murphy, 1853.

Green, J. R.—*History of the English People,* American Book Co., 1916.

Grotius, Hugo—*De Jure Belli et Pacis,* Trans. by A. C. Campbell, London, Walter Dunne, 1901.

Guizot, M.—History of the Origin of Representative Government in Europe, London, Henry G. Bohn, 1861. *History of Civilization in Europe,* New York, D. Appleton & Co., 1896.

Hallam, Henry—*The Middle Ages,* 2 vols., New York, D. Appleton, 1904.

Hergenrother, J. K. (Kirsh, J. P.)—*Handbuch der Kirchengeschichte,* 4 vols., St Louis, Herder, 1916.

Hobbes, Thomas—*Leviathan,* London, Henry Morley Ed., 1887

Holland, F. M.—*Rise of Intellectual Liberty,* New York, Holt 1885.

Holt, L. H.—*Introduction to the Study of Government,* New York, Macmillan, 1919.

Holzwarth, J. F.—*Weltgeschichte.* VII vols., Franz Hirschheim, Mainz, 1887.

Hooker, Richard—*Laws of Ecclesiastical Polity,* Book V, *Theory of Church and State,* Book VII, New York, Appelton, 1857.

Hunt, Gaillard— "Virginia Declaration of Rights and Cardinal Bellarmine," *Catholic Historical Review,* October, 1917.

Janssen, Johnnes—*Geschichte des Deutschen Volkes,* Herder, St. Louis, 1883.

Jenks, Edward—*Law and Politics in the Middle Ages*, New York Holt, 1898.

Kurth, Godfrey—*The Church at the Turning Points of History,* Trans. by Rt. Rev. Victor Day, 1918, Naegel Printing Co., Helena, Montana.

Laski, Harold J.—*Studies in the Problem of Sovereignty,* New Haven, Yale University Press, 1917.

Lavisse, Ernest, and Rambaud, A.—*Histoire Générale,* Paris Colin, 1893.

Larence, T. J.--*Principles of International Law,* Boston, D. C. Health & Co., 1900.

Le Bachelet, Xavier-Marie, S. J.—*Auctarium Bellarminianurm,* Paris, Gabriel Beauchesne, 1913.

Lecky, W. E. H.—*History of European Morals,* 2 vols., 1889, *Rationalism in Europe,* 2 vols., 1882, *Democracy and Liberty,* 2 vols., 1882, Appleton, New York.

Leo XIII, Pope -- "Immortale Dei."

Lingard, John—*History of England,* Baltimore, Murphy, 1876.

Locke, John—*Two Treatises of Civil Government,* London, George Routledge, 1884.

Lucas, Rev. H.— "Democracy in Theory and Practice," *Month*, Nov. 1920.

Maine, Henry Summer—*International Law,* New York, Henry Holt & Co., 1888.

Masterson, E.— "Origin of Civil Authority," *Irish Theological Quarterly,* April, 1921.

Morris, H. F.—*History of Development of Constitutional & Civil Liberty,* Washington, D. C., 1898.

Montague, F. C.—*Political History of England* (1603-1660), New York, Macmillan, 1907.

Montesquieu, Baron de --*Esprit Des Lois*, Paris, 1877.

Munro, D. C. and Seller, G. C.—*Mediaeval Civilization,* New York, The Century Co, 1904. *The Middle Ages*, New York, The Century Co.

Murphy, Edward --*St. Thomas' Political Doctrine and Democracy,* Catholic University, Washington, D. C. 1921.

O'Rahilly, Alfred— "Catholic Origin of Democray," *Studies,* March, 1919. "Sources of English and American Democracy," Studies, June, 1919. "Sovereignty of the People," *Studies,* March and June 1921. "Democracy of St. Thomas," *Studies,* March, 1920. "Suarez and Democracy," *Studies,* March, 1918. "Democracy, Parliament and Cromwell," *Studies,* Dec., 1918. "Some Theology on Tyranny," *Irish Theological Quarterly,* Oct., 1920.

Pierers—*Konversations Lexikon,* Stuttgart, 1893.

Pius X, Pope—"Motu Proprio," *Christian Democracy,* Catholic Truth Society, London.

Raitz v. Frentz, S. J. --*Der Ehrwürdige Kardinal Robert Bellarmine, S.J.,* Freiburg im Breisgau, 1921, Herder and Co., St. Louis.

Rolbiecki, John Joseph—*Political Philosophy of Dante,* Washington, D. C. Catholic University, 1921.

Ryan, Dr. John A.—*Right of Self-Government,* New York, Paulist Press, 1920. "Nature of the State," *America,* July 2, 1921. *Distributive Justice,* New York, 1919.

Seignobos, Charles—*History of Mediavel and Modern Civilization,* New York, Charles Scribner's Sons, 1907.

Shahan, Thomas J.—*The Middle Ages,* Cincinnati, Benziger, 1904.

Smith, A.L.--*Church and State in the Middle Ages,* Oxford, Clarendon, 1903.

Stille´, C. J.—*Studies in Mediaeval History,* Philadelphia, Lippincott, 1882.

Stubbs, William--*Constitutional History of England,* 3 volumes, 1897-1903.

Taparelli, D. Azeglio-*Cours Elémentaire de Droit Natureal,* Tournai, 1863.

Taylor, H.O.-- *The Mediaevel Mind,* 2 volumes, New York, Macmillan, 1911.

Taylor, Hannis --*The Origin and Growth of the American Constitution,* Boston and New York, 1911.

Thomas, St.—*Summa Theologica,* Romae, Forzani et S., 1894, *De Regimine Principum,* Opuscula Naples, 1849.

Tocqueville, Alexis De—*La Démocratie en Amérique*, 2 vols., Paris, 1874.

Turner, William—*History of Philosophy*, New York, Ginn & Company, 1903.

Vareilles-Somnuéres—*Principes Fondamentaux du Droit*, Paris, 1889.

Walsh, James J.—*The Thirteenth, Greatest of Centuries*, Catholic Summer School Press, New York, 1913.

Wetzer and Welte—*Kirchenlexicon*, Freiburg, i. B., 1897.

Willoughby, W. W.—*An Examination of the State*, New York, Macmillan, 1896.

Wilson, Woodrow—*Congressional Government*, Boston, Houghton, Mifflin, 1885. *The State*, Boston, D. C., Heath & Co., 1903.

Woolsey, Theodore D.—*Political Science or the State*, 2 vols., New York, Charles Scribner's Sons, 1893.

Morton Arboretum Biking and Hiking

12

LISLE

TRAIL LENGTH

4.8 miles for bicycling (arboretum members only) and 14 miles of hiking trails.

TRAIL SURFACE

The narrow asphalt roadway is open for bicycling on the east side of the Morton Arboretum. Bikes are not allowed off the road or on any other trails.

Meadow Lake has a paved 0.6-mile hiking trail that is flat and accessible for people that are mobility challenged. Another paved hiking or strolling path extends for one mile from the Visitor Center to the arboretum's west side and across the West Branch of the DuPage River bridge to the Thornhill building. It is somewhat of a steep climb up to the Thornhill building.

There are more than twelve miles of wood-chipped, turf and dirt pathways throughout the 1,700-acre Morton Arboretum. Trails are looped and out and back routes that wind their way thru extensive plant collections and landscape exhibits.

DIRECTIONS

Located at 4100 Illinois Route 53 the main entrance is at Park Avenue on the east side of Illinois Route 53 in Lisle. The entrance is one-half mile north of the Interstate 88 tollway on the east side of Illinois Route 53 and south of Butterfield Road (Illinois Route 56).

TRAILHEAD LOCATIONS

Morton Arboretum members who want to bicycle on the east side road system must park their cars at the main parking lot on the east side.

Hikers can take their pick of parking areas located along the road system.

Trail Description

Visitors can hike the more than fourteen miles of trail or ride the 4.8-mile east side road system at the 1,700-acre arboretum. There are more than 3,400 plant species from fifty-nine different countries to view, smell, touch and learn about. The road system used for biking is a closed loop through the east side's oak, pine, elm, and maple collections. Beside the fresh smells of pine trees bike riders will see a beautiful marsh, Crabapple Lake, Meadow Lake and many northern Illinois native plants and animals. The bicycling road system is asphalt paved and it has a gently rolling topography suitable for a most family friendly excursion.

Portions of the hiking trails are paved and easily accessed by people of all abilities. Other sections are narrow turf or wood-chipped trails that meander and curl through the woods and prairie. The beautiful woodlands, prairie, wetlands, small lakes, the East Branch of the DuPage River and glorious gardens feature globally rare and native plant materials. Many seasonal explorations are highlighted by the arboretum's staff member tours, special weekend events and Web site descriptions.

Traveler's Notebook

Visitors must pay an admission fee or join as a member. The relaxing bike rides are open to Morton Arboretum members only on Friday and Saturday evenings from 5 p.m. to 9 p.m., May through August. The roadway is narrow and helmets are strongly recommended. The offering is intended for families and those who want to take a cruising ride and coast to observe the beauty of nature and plant collections along the way. Helmets are strongly recommended if not required.

The grounds are open every day of the year from 7 a.m. until 5 p.m. during Central Standard Time and from 7 a.m. until 7 p.m. during daylight savings time. The arboretum prohibits alcohol, pets, grilling, active sports and bicycles (except for members at designated times). The Morton Arboretum provides a safe secure atmosphere for visitors.

Trail Talk

With more than 3,400 types of trees, shrubs and other plants here you can have a bloomin' good time in the spring or a spectacular fall color exploration. All seasons can be enjoyed and the museum staff members make it fun and easy to learn about the collections and get involved in a program, self-guided or guided tour. There are many special events and instructional programs offered to homeowners, families, children, landscape professionals and gardeners throughout the year.

Volunteers assist with all phases of the operation and they are an appreciated human resource that is an essential component that helps to make the Morton Arboretum one of the best outdoor museums on the planet. It is an interesting and enjoyable place to visit with always something different going on or several new varieties of plants to look at and learn about. The Arboretum is a good place to support by joining as a member and then you can ride and hike to your heart's content.

Once you join you can also dine in the Ginkgo Café, visit the Sterling Morton Library or ask the experts questions about ailing plants at the Plant Clinic. One of the most striking landscapes a visitor can witness is Daffodil Glade when it is in full bloom. Other highlights include the Schulenberg

Prairie restoration project, the flowering crabapple trees and placid beauty of the small lakes offering nature's reflections.

Joy Morton was the founder of Morton Salt Company and the son of the founder of Arbor Day. The Morton Arboretum was established in 1922 to promote conservation and study of trees and plants. There are tree and shrub collections from fifty-nine countries. Mae Watts, the naturalist who first proposed the idea of setting aside the Chicago, Aurora and Elgin Railroad property as a path way (which became the Illinois Prairie Path), worked here for many years.

FOR MORE INFORMATION

Visit the website at www.mortonarb.org or telephone (630) 719-2400.

Photo courtesy of Morton Arboretum.

Oldfield Oaks Forest Preserve Trail

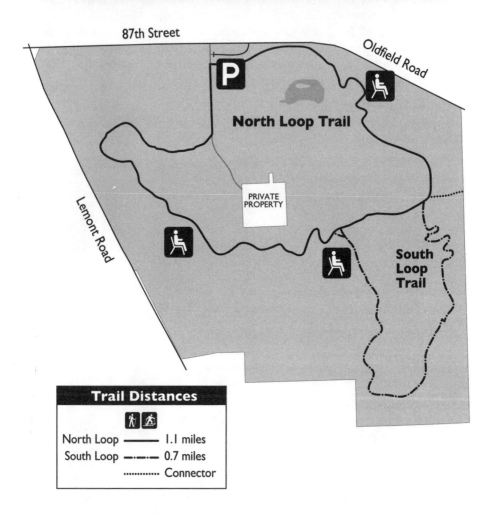

87th Street

Oldfield Road

P

North Loop Trail

PRIVATE PROPERTY

South Loop Trail

Lemont Road

Trail Distances

North Loop	——————	1.1 miles
South Loop	—·—·—	0.7 miles
	··········	Connector